HOW TO BE AN ONLINE TUTOR

To Jimmy, Blanche and Esme

HOW TO BE AN ONLINE TUTOR

Julia Duggleby

Gower

Published by
Gower Publishing Limited
Gower House
Croft Road
Aldershot
Hampshire GU11 3HR
England

Gower
Old Post Road
Brookfield
Vermont 05036
USA

Julia Duggleby has asserted her right under the Copyright, Designs and Patents Act 1988 to be identified as the author of this work.

British Library Cataloguing in Publication Data
Duggleby, Julia
    How to be an online tutor
    1. Computer-assisted instruction 2. Distance education –
    Computer-assisted instruction 3. Information storage and
    retrieval systems – User education 4. Tutors and tutoring
    I. Title
    374.2'6

    ISBN 0 566 08247 0

Library of Congress Cataloging-in-Publication Data
Duggleby, Julia.
    How to be an online tutor/Julia Duggleby.
        p. cm.
    Includes bibliographical references (p.).
    ISBN 0-566-08247-0 (hard)
    1. Education—Data processing. 2. Internet (Computer network) in
    education. 3. Tutors and tutoring. I. Title.

    LB1044.87 .D84 2000
    371.39'4 21—dc21   99-044902

Typeset in Plantin Light by Bournemouth Colour Press, Parkstone and printed in Great Britain by Cambridge University Press.

CONTENTS

LIST OF FIGURES

FOREWARD

I have always derived great personal satisfaction from seeing the pleasure on people's faces when they learn new things and rise to challenges. This vicarious pleasure has fuelled my interest in learning for all of my working career, even when my involvement in the learning of others has been at a distance. I am also tremendously excited by technology developments. Such developments have the ability to improve the way we live, work and play. So what would be better than coming across a book on being an online tutor that combines two great interests of mine, better use of technology and improving the way that people learn together? It is an even greater pleasure to realise that this book is written by someone who is not a technofreak. In Julia's words, she came to technology late in life. Thus the book is written to make technology and its use for learning very transparent to those readers to whom the phrase 'online' sounds like a fish caught on a hook. Also the book is written, as Julia says, from her direct experience. I can confirm the value of the course, not from direct experience but because several of my colleagues from Lloyds TSB Training did the LeTTOL course and got a lot from it. The approach has value for corporate training, I can vouch for that, but it also has value to the further and higher education sectors being developed by the South Yorkshire FE Colleges' Consortium. Whatever your background, this book will be valuable if you intend to design online materials or support learners learning online. This book brings together everything that the online tutor needs to consider. By the way, even if you have no intention of being an online tutor, you will want to use the Internet for your own learning by the time you have finished this book.

The UK learning industry is worth about £8 billion, most of it spent and consumed within the UK. Online learning gives the UK a huge opportunity to increase the efficiency with which everyone learns and to make our expertise in learning available worldwide. Julia tutors on a course that includes learners living and working in

Australia, Canada and Singapore. This is a first-hand account of how to make global online learning work at a practical hands-on level.

Why should this be so important at this time? Firstly, the rise and rise of the Internet is changing the way we shop and communicate. It is so much cheaper to send an e-mail than either a fax or a letter. You can shop worldwide from home and have material delivered within a few days. What is more natural than changing the way we learn as well? However, learning is a social experience and will always be so. Learning happens all the time and in so many different ways: classroom study, reading, working alongside an expert, television and radio, doing (and making mistakes) and observing others. Learning is something that involves others as well as the learner; the encouragement of family and friends is part of the learning experience. The online tutor has a very specific and vital role to play in the future of learning. The perception many have of online learning is that it is a lonely and solitary experience and that it takes place away from the real job and real people. This has led to the comment that learning through technology is not real learning. Nothing could be further from the truth. Getting it right for the future is important, and this book will help you in that process.

Secondly, if each one of us is to retain skills that are valuable in the global market place and thereby retain our current high standard of living, then we have to offer a higher added value in our skill set. We can only do this if we constantly update and improve our skill set. Learning has to become a routine and commonplace work activity that is delivered at an ever-decreasing cost for each one of us. We can do that by adding the human element into online learning as well as excellent design of our learning materials. A recent study by the Institute of Management confirms that the office as a social environment is one of the major reasons for turning up to work. The Institute recently completed a detailed study of the working habits and attitudes of 1 312 of its members. Pleasure in relationships with colleagues was cited as the cause of greatest satisfaction relating to work. The needs of individuals must be taken into account when implementing new ways of learning. Learning is a social activity and we must deliver learning to a social environment. We can no longer afford to do that in classrooms away from people's workplaces and homes.

Having experienced and successful online tutors will help in improving the efficiency of learning as well as helping many more people acquire new skills.

An important outcome of successful online tutoring is to encourage individuals to take responsibility for their own development. The online tutor must provide a climate in which people will take responsibility for their learning. Again in Julia's words; the role of an online tutor is to guide learners through the course so that they complete it successfully. Online learners have complete access to and control over all the component parts of the course material and much else that they can obtain elsewhere. The tutor has a role as a facilitator of learning, leaving the technology and other learners to deliver the content.

Howard Hills, BA FIPD
Deputy Chairman of the Forum for Technology in Training

THE FORUM FOR TECHNOLOGY IN TRAINING

The Forum for Technology in Training was founded in 1982 with the objectives of 'promoting performance improvement through the greater and more effective use of technology in training and development' and 'enabling members to meet and exchange experience and views for their mutual benefit'.

Members of the Forum are drawn from a diversity of organizations, including major users, in most industry sectors as well as government and the armed forces, together with suppliers, academics, independent consultants and ancillary services.

The five meetings a year allow members to meet, network, share ideas and hear about developments in technology-based training.

For more information on the Forum, its services and membership, contact:

Brian Tucker
The Forum for Technology in Training
Orchard Chambers
4 Rocky Lane
Heswall
Wirral
CH60 0BY
Tel: 0151 342 8606
Fax: 0151 342 1660

ACKNOWLEDGEMENTS

I must offer my thanks to:

- the Learning to Teach On-line development and tutor team on whose work this book is based, principally Shirley Chartron (Rother Valley College), Jo Kirby and Fred Pickering (Barnsley College) and Seb Schmoller (The Sheffield College);
- Irshad Akbar, South Yorkshire Colleges' Consortium Coordinator, for behind the scenes support;
- my colleagues at the Sheffield College who are also involved in using the Internet for teaching and who have provided me with advice and ideas: Dave Pickersgill, Tony Fletcher, Richard Moore, Viv Drake and David Levine;
- Ken Ruddiman, Principal of the Sheffield College, for backing me in this project;
- Learning to Teach On-line students, past and present, who have been such a pleasure to teach, who have shown such enthusiasm for our course, and from whom I have learned so much.

I would also like to thank the following organizations for permission to reproduce the figures:

- Netscape Communications Corporation for Netscape Navigator (Portions Copyright Netscape Communications Corporation, 1998. All Rights Reserved. Netscape, Netscape Navigator and the Netscape N Logo are registered trademarks of Netscape in the United States and other countries.)
- Microsoft Corporation for Microsoft Internet Explorer (Screen shot(s) reprinted by permission from Microsoft Corporation.)
- O'Reilly & Associates, Inc. for WebBoard (Reprinted with permission from O'Reilly & Associates, Inc. For orders and information call 800-998-9938.)

INTRODUCTION

Five years ago only a few people would have even heard of the Internet, let alone known what it was, or would have made regular use of it. Yet it is now transforming the way that human beings find things out, shop, work, play and communicate with one another. Included in that transformation is the way in which we can teach and learn. This book will show you – the tutor, trainer, lecturer or teacher – how to be part of that transformation.

I came to information and communications technology relatively late in life, when I treated myself to my first personal computer on my forty-fifth birthday. I bought my computer mainly with the intention of using it as a word processor, but the system included a modem, albeit ludicrously slow by today's standards, which gave me access to e-mail and the Web. It was a revelation and I was fascinated and amazed by this wonderful new resource and its potential. In those early days receiving an e-mail was a rare treat. I spent a year joining discussion lists, trying to find friends who also had e-mail with whom I could correspond, and creating a web site for a community group with which I was involved. The college that employs me was beginning to think about developing Living IT, a suite of online courses which would teach people how to use the Internet effectively. With my barely sufficient technical understanding, and tremendous enthusiasm, I became involved in the design and delivery of one of those courses. This involvement led me into the college's next online venture, Learning to Teach On-line (LeTTOL – <http://www.sheffcol.ac.uk/lettol/>), an online course developed by a consortium of South Yorkshire colleges which would in its first phase build up the online skills of the region's further education tutors. My role this time was as a student in the pilot course. Again I loved it and in the second pilot run I was elevated to a tutor role, and have been tutoring on this course ever since. The course has expanded considerably and has included students from as far beyond the boundaries of South Yorkshire as Australia, Canada and Singapore.

This book has arisen out of my experience as a student and tutor on the LeTTOL course and as a tutor on Living IT and its aim is to be a practical guide to anyone thinking of developing online courses. It assumes that you, the reader, have little in the way of technical expertise – perhaps some experience of the World Wide Web and e-mail, but no more. It is not intended to be a technical manual but may help you improve your technical knowledge as well as your pedagogical understanding.

The book also assumes that you have some experience of teaching and training but that you want some guidance about how you can translate what you do to an online environment, either in the conversion of existing courses or in the creation of new courses.

Although the book's main focus is on delivering courses entirely online, there is plenty of useful information in it for anyone who wishes to use the Internet to enhance the face-to-face courses they teach.

The book is divided into five parts:

I   What is online learning, who wants it and why?
II   A tutor's guide to the Internet
III The planning cycle
IV   Getting your course up and running
V   Appendices

PART *I*

What is online learning, who wants it and why?

1 DIFFERENT MODES FOR DELIVERING LEARNING?

In order to provide some context to a book about online teaching and learning it will be helpful to start by briefly pinning down some of the terms that are used when describing different modes of delivery of learning and then to see how online learning fits in. In the next chapter I will explore some of the issues and challenges arising from these delivery modes, particularly distance education, and how online learning can address some of the drawbacks of both face-to-face and distance education.

Face to face

Face to face is the most traditional form of delivering education, and the one with which people will have had direct experience since mainstream schooling throughout the world is taught in this way. Face-to-face education is teaching and learning where a significant component requires the presence of both learner and tutor in the same physical space at the same time. The definition includes such activities as lectures, demonstrations, tutorials, presentations and seminars. It is likely that a course delivered primarily face to face will also have some elements that involve independent study, such as supplementary reading, research and writing of assignments. As a general rule as learners mature, and as their study skills become more sophisticated, the ratio of independent to classroom-based study increases. However, tutors and students are not likely to be based very far apart geographically and regular timetabled meetings between tutor and student allow learners to access support as they need it. So this would still fall within the definition of face-to-face education.

Open learning

Open learning has been developed in recent years to allow learners more flexibility than they would normally encounter in a face-to-face course. Learners attend some sort of learning centre at times that suit them and work through course materials at their own pace. They will still meet up with a tutor, perhaps on a regular basis or perhaps on request, and may have access to additional support whilst in the learning centre. Open learning has often been used to enable learners to develop core skills such as literacy and numeracy, information technology and study skills.

Traditional distance education

This term is used to describe teaching and learning situations where the significant component does not require the presence of both learner and tutor in the same physical space at the same time. For the most part the time, pace and location of the learning is determined by the learner. The teaching is delivered using correspondence, books and other paper-based materials, increasingly supplemented by audio-visual materials such as video and TV, and by radio. Indeed there may be some element of computer-enhanced learning, for example in the use of CD-Roms. It may be that occasionally events are organized that do involve a same time/same place interaction, such as tutorials or a summer school.

Online learning

Online learning is a kind of distance education, but it makes considerable use of information and communications technologies such as e-mail, Internet conferencing and the World Wide Web. Course materials can be mounted on to a web site. Speedy interactions can take place between tutor and learner using e-mail, and, perhaps most significantly of all, collaboration between learners can easily take place, allowing for the building of a learning community which allows learners to work and socialize together, as they would in a face-to-face course. It has been said that online learning takes the 'distance' out of 'distance education'.

As will be clear from these broad definitions, hard and fast distinctions do not exist between the different modes of delivery of learning but these definitions will give some idea of what is meant by the terms when I use them in this book.

2 WHY CHOOSE ONLINE LEARNING AND FOR WHOM?

The impact of technology on distance education

PRE-TWENTIETH CENTURY

As will be seen, distance education is by no means a new idea. It can be argued that its history goes back thousands of years when voyagers travelled the world and transported with them their systems of beliefs, their skills in navigation, boat building and architecture, and their social structures. In most cases this 'education' would be spread by word of mouth, by example, or be imposed upon a reluctant host culture. There might be little written down and if it was such writing would be unlikely to be produced in multiple copies. There is only one Rosetta Stone and if there were more they would be rather cumbersome to distribute. So it is the progress of technology that has allowed for the easier reproduction and distribution of information and that in its turn has impacted on the development of distance education.

As soon as information could be disseminated to a mass audience then distance education could take place, and thus distance education can be counted as beginning with the development of Gutenberg's printing press, which provided the technology for widespread distribution. More recently the postal service has allowed communication to take place between separated tutor and student. The first instance of a correspondence course is in the nineteenth century, when Isaac Pitman realized that the universal postal services would enable him to deliver the teaching of shorthand to a wider audience.

TWENTIETH CENTURY

Correspondence courses became more widespread in the twentieth century and continue to be popular to this day. However, in the second half of the century new technologies began to be used to supplement and enhance paper-based materials. Here are some examples:

- 1951 – In Australia two-way radio was used for tutor/student communication by the Alice Springs School of the Air.
- 1960s – Telephone conferencing was used by the University of Wisconsin to supplement paper-based learning materials.
- 1970s – The Open University of Great Britain was established, which allowed people to study for degrees without physically attending a university. The Open University used paper-based materials, and also radio, TV and, later, video to supplement these. It proved phenomenally successful.

Why distance learning?

The popularity of traditional distance education in the twentieth century shows that it has fulfilled a need for many people. There are a variety of reasons for its popularity.

- It gives access to a wide range of knowledge, skills and qualifications.
- People who find it difficult to commit themselves to regular time slots, such as people who work shifts, can study whenever they want, day or night.
- People whose work involves travel away from home can take their coursework with them wherever they happen to be.
- Courses can be undertaken by people who have a multiplicity of commitments and demands on their time, such as those caring for young children or in full-time employment.
- It allows people who live in remote areas to study, even where there are no local educational institutions.
- Time isn't wasted in travelling to an institution, finding a parking place or waiting for a bus.
- People who have disabilities that prevent or deter them from accessing face-to-face education can participate.
- Students can choose for themselves the best time to embark on a new course.
- In many cases progress through the course can be at a pace

determined by the student and can be compressed into a few weeks or spread over years.

- It may prove a cheaper option for students since money can be saved on fares and on childcare costs.
- Students can work towards higher qualifications without loss of income because they do not have to leave employment.
- Specialist courses that may not be available locally can be undertaken.
- Distance learning materials, such as text books, video and audio, usually have a high standard of content and presentation.
- The quality of teaching may be less dependent on the skills of the teacher.
- Students can be judged by the quality of their work alone – prejudice based on their class, ethnicity, age or speech is less likely.

There are advantages, too, for the organization offering distance education:

- Specialist courses can be offered that would not otherwise be viable if they could only be undertaken by local people.
- Savings can be made on accommodation (including cleaning, lighting and heating of rooms) and student services such as refectories.

However, distance education has clear disadvantages:

- Students may feel socially isolated and so may find it more difficult to stay motivated.
- There are few opportunities for students to develop their ideas through discussion with others on the course.
- Student collaboration on specific tasks is not possible.
- There is no peer group support.
- There may be little flexibility in the content of the course.
- Learning materials that have been expensive to develop may quickly go out of date.
- Feedback from tutors is slow and students may have to wait weeks to find out if their work is meeting the required standards.
- Clarifications and queries cannot be dealt with speedily.
- Misunderstandings may not come to light and be quickly cleared up.
- Tutors cannot 'read' body language and so are unlikely to detect boredom or confusion.

- Since distance education is primarily text based, a high level of literacy is necessary.
- Some subjects need specialist equipment that may be expensive for students to own, or impossible to obtain.
- It may be difficult to teach certain practical skills.

Is online learning the answer?

It is clear that there is a big demand for distance education and that it provides a high quality of teaching and learning to many people. It is also clear that distance education has serious shortcomings both for the tutor and the student. Can online learning resolve, or at least mitigate, the disadvantages of distance education? Yes, it can, and this is how.

Communication is quick

- A communication between tutor and student that may have once taken weeks to transact by post can be completed in a few hours.
- Students will enjoy speedy feedback on completed assignments.
- Clarification can be easily made, and points of confusion more simply resolved.

Communication is of a high quality

- Students who may be too shy to ask questions in class may feel more comfortable using e-mail.
- Tutor/student communication is individualized.

Student interaction can take place

- E-mail is easy – messages can be sent and responded to within minutes, and mailing groups can be set up so that e-mailing 15 people takes no longer than e-mailing one person.
- This means that communication between students becomes practicable.
- Exercises and activities that involve collaboration, such as discussion, pair work and group tasks, can be incorporated into the learning.
- Social interactions and peer support can take place.
- Courses can incorporate conferencing software that further facilitates debate, discussion, collaboration and social communications.

- Real time (synchronous) communication can be introduced using Chat facilities and video- or telephone-conferencing.

Development and maintenance of learning materials is easy

- Web-based materials are cheap and quick to produce and need not require a high level of technical expertise.
- These materials can be of very high quality, and can easily incorporate colourful text and graphics.
- As the technology becomes faster, more stable and more sophisticated then sound, video and animations can be exchanged with ease.
- Web materials can be amended, added to and uploaded in minutes ensuring that the content is always accurate, up to date and relevant.
- The materials can be constantly reviewed and revised in the light of student feedback.
- There is no need for the providing institution to reproduce and distribute learning materials.

Online courses are widely accessible

- Computer and Internet technology is becoming cheaper and ownership more widespread.
- There are increasing opportunities for people to get on to the Internet even if they cannot access at home – Internet-linked computers can be found at work, in libraries, in cybercafes and in community centres.
- Students from a wide mix of backgrounds, countries and cultures can take part.

Who are our potential learners?

What sort of students are likely to be attracted to online courses? Well, naturally, they will need to have access to a computer that is connected to the Internet, and they will need the know-how to use it. Most of your students will be those who find it inconvenient or impossible to access a course face to face, and you will certainly find that they are willing to try out studying in a technologically innovative way.

Here are a few snapshots of people who might feel that an online course is for them.

Jim Buchanan

The situation Jim is a single parent with two daughters, both in primary school. He was an unskilled worker in the steel industry but was made redundant. He supplements his small income from state benefits by being the junior school's lollipop man. He would like to find a full-time job now his daughters are old enough to go to the after-school club.

The problem Jim's lollipop job means that he has to be on duty twice a day, and this makes getting to a day course an impossibility. He cannot join an evening class because he hasn't got anyone to look after his daughters. He needs a job that will give him time off during school holidays. He hasn't got a computer and he can't afford one.

The solution Jim finds out that there is an online course that could train him as a classroom assistant. The school his children attend is keen on parental involvement and the headteacher agrees that he can access the school's computer. He will 'pay' for this privilege by going into the school once a week to help with reading. This will also provide him with additional relevant experience.

Sobia Khan

The situation Sobia is employed as a clerical worker in a cricket bat factory in Islamabad. She has good IT skills and is enthusiastic about computers. Her employer thinks that he could sell more cricket bats if he advertised on the Internet.

The problem Neither Sobia nor her employer knows much about the Internet. Sobia's employer is worried that Sobia may be looking for another job which will be more interesting and perhaps pay better. Sobia is reluctant to go to college because the nearest one is a long way from her home and anyway her employer worries that if she goes to college each week then the factory will not be able to cope with orders at busy times.

The solution Sobia's employer finds out that Sobia could do courses about using the Internet online. He invests in an Internet connection and Sobia does a course which introduces her to the Internet and follows this up with a course on web authoring. As a course assignment she builds a web site for the cricket bat factory. She can study at work when she has time, and when the factory isn't too busy. She enjoys the course so much that she stops looking for another job. The web site she builds attracts custom, the factory expands and Sobia is promoted to a more senior and better paid position.

Tanya Silver

The situation Tanya is an elderly lady with a very lively mind. She enjoyed great academic success as a young woman, and had a career as a biochemist. Now she is retired she would like to learn more about art as she feels that this is a neglected side of her education.

The problem Tanya suffers from severe arthritis and cannot attend a course, or use a keyboard or mouse with ease.

The solution Tanya has heard of online learning and decides to investigate further. She discovers that she could use a computer without having to use her hands a great deal since it is possible to adapt the keyboard and mouse, and to use voice recognition software. She obtains a secondhand computer and gets a small grant from a charity for the elderly to have the necessary adaptions done, goes online and finds an Art History and Appreciation course. Not only does she love the course, but she finds herself communicating daily with a wide circle of new friends from around the world.

Clive Woodhead

The situation Clive teaches French and German to teenagers at a school in the middle of a suburban housing estate with high unemployment. The schoolchildren he teaches rarely leave their estate, let alone travel to Europe. Clive is feeling demotivated and stressed.

The problem Clive cannot afford to leave teaching. He also feels that as he is over 50 finding a new job would be difficult.

The solution Clive hears about an online course that teaches how to tutor online and he signs up. He realizes that he could develop a small business and sets up an enterprise tutoring French online to business people. This business brings him just enough income to allow him to continue working as a schoolteacher, but he can reduce his hours to half time. He finds that his experience with the Internet can also be used to enhance his classroom delivery. He forges links with schools in Germany and France. Both he and his students become more motivated. Clive starts to enjoy his work for the first time in years.

SOME STATISTICS

The Graphics, Visualization & Usability (GVU) Center at Georgia Tech conducts a regular World Wide Web User Survey which makes interesting reading. Trends in the survey published in January 1999 show that women are in a minority internationally (38.5 per cent) though this is a considerable rise from 1994 when only 5.1 per cent of women were users. Internet users are generally better educated with more than 50 per cent having a first degree, though as web access expands education attainment levels are decreasing and becoming more in line with the general population. Annual income levels are going down too – again a trend that suggests an interest in the Internet from the wider population. More than 90 per cent have English as their primary language, though bear in mind that the survey was only available in English. The average age is 35 and this is rising. The majority of users live in the United States (84 per cent) with the second biggest group in Europe (6 per cent). Education is the occupational field with the most users (26 per cent), with computing coming in second at 22 per cent. The growth of new users of the Internet seems to have slowed a little, and new users are more likely to be either in the under 20 or in the over 50 age group. The majority of web users access from home, and it is home- rather than work-based users that appear to be growing the fastest. The survey also asked what were respondents' primary uses of the Web and education did well, coming in at third place, after personal information and entertainment.

For the online tutor the trend that seems to be the most interesting is the move towards a less elite group on the Internet – people with a lower annual income and a lower level of educational attainment. These are people who may well wish to improve their educational level and indeed regard the Internet as a resource for education. What is more, the survey also found that the items most often purchased over the Internet were books and magazines.

Statistics such as these, though fascinating, must be treated with some caution since this survey was more likely to have got a response from those who use the Web regularly. However, they most certainly show that Internet use is growing, and growing amongst people who may well wish to access the Internet in order to learn online. Good news for the online tutor.

And who are the potential providers?

It seems clear that there are plenty of people with access to the Internet who are interested in learning online. Who might provide them with these opportunities?

UNIVERSITIES AND COLLEGES

Already there is large scale provision in the United States and Canada of online courses at all educational levels. This is no doubt partly fuelled by the fact that these countries are the most advanced in terms of Internet access. However, it is clear their lead is being followed now by the rest of the world.

OTHER EDUCATIONAL PROVIDERS

There have always been other providers of education, both face to face and distance, and these too are seeing the potential of delivering online. Such organizations as the BBC, the British Council and the National Extension College have all started to provide some online courses. Since offering a course has relatively low overheads, individuals with a particular expertise can reasonably consider providing an online course.

STAFF TRAINERS

Large organizations such as businesses, governments and charities have always been aware of the need to train their staff to carry out their job roles. Many are now putting into place training that can be delivered online, thus saving on the expense of providing travel and accommodation for staff attending courses. It has also become possible for such organizations to easily access the exact training they need using organizations anywhere in the world.

PART II

A tutor's guide to the Internet

3 INTRODUCTION TO THE INTERNET

What is the Internet?

The Internet consists of millions of computers, all linked together by telephone lines, cable and satellite. And between them these computers hold many more millions of pages of information – I don't know how many now but whatever figure I put down on paper today will be out of date by the end of the week. As a rough guide, let us just say there are about 320 million pages. That's an awful lot of information.

And how many people have regular access to all this information? Again the rate of growth is so fast that the figure I put here will be wrong in a week. Let us say about 140 million people.

The Internet is a massive library. It is the biggest library that has ever existed and also one that you can pop into with a few mouse clicks or keyboard strokes. It is a library that you can reach from your workplace, from your home, from the place where you study – and possibly from your local library.

What sort of library is it? In a library you would expect to find text and pictures, and perhaps most modern libraries would also have a stock of audio-visual materials – videos, tapes and compact discs. The Internet can provide that too – billions of words plus photographs, voices, songs, animations and video (though I admit the technology will need a bit more development before full length feature films will be accessible on the Internet).

But beyond a certain point the library analogy ceases to work because the Internet is not only a source of textual, visual and aural information, but also an interactive medium. You can do things on the Internet – you can talk to people, exchange ideas, buy things, ask questions, play games, apply for jobs. So as well as being a library it is also a party and a funfair and a debating chamber and a post office and an employment agency and a marketplace. And, as we will see, it is a tutorial room, a seminar, a classroom, a lecture hall, a refectory and a common room.

The growth of the Internet has provided an information and communications revolution that has changed the world. The effect of its development on the way we find things out, and communicate with one another, will have as great an impact as the invention of the printing press.

And all this without getting up off your bottom!

Let's look at some examples of how the Internet can be used today (and don't worry if you don't understand all the terms – you will by the end of this book).

> **Fred and Georgia** have been married 20 years and think they would like a treat. Their mutual interest is art. They look at the tourist information pages of various European cities and find out there is an exhibition of Goya's work in Madrid in August, and of Rembrandt's work in The Hague in July. They love both artists, but a comparison of typical temperatures for each city makes them decide on The Hague. Using the tourist information site again they get details of 5-star hotels (this is a treat remember). They use an online form to book the hotel over the Internet and get confirmation by e-mail within three hours. They compare various travel agents' sites and find a flight at the time and price they want, and book that too. They contact their bank (yes, on the Internet) and order currency. They then amuse themselves for a couple of hours finding out as much as they can about Rembrandt's life and work, planning day trips from The Hague using an online timetable, and arguing about who's turn it is to make the coffee (coffee-making not yet a service easily available on the Internet).
>
> **Vikram** is editing a (hardcopy) newsletter for an international bird protection organization. This is the first time he has edited this newsletter so he starts off by downloading a newsletter template from the Internet. He then e-mails some of the supporters of the organization and asks them for articles. Within 12 hours he has received (as attachments) one article from Malaysia and

another from Peru, and others arrive soon after.
Meanwhile he has done some research on the Golden
Eagle, written an article and found some (copyright free)
photographs that he can use. He downloads some photo-
editing software because he wants to enhance the photos
before including them in the newsletter. He likes this new
software and decides he will buy it (using e-mail) after the
30-day evaluation period. Once the newsletter is done he
e-mails it as an attachment to the editorial board for
comment. He also decides that he is going to learn about
web authoring because he wants the next newsletter to be
available on the Internet as it would save considerably on
postage costs (as well as reach a lot more people).

Maria is a sociology student at her local college. She
suffers from multiple sclerosis and this means that
occasionally she is too ill to attend college. She has an
assignment to do on lone parents, but her legs are weak at
the moment so she e-mails her tutor who e-mails back her
lecture notes and a list of web sites that she could use to
find out more. The college has set up a conference facility
for learners and Maria can go online and exchange ideas
on the topic with other learners on the course. Maria
completes the assignment and e-mails it to her tutor within
the deadline. (By the way, one of the other learners rather
likes Maria but was too shy to ask her out in person so
instead sent her an e-mail card asking for a date – Maria
agreed.)

George is the health and safety officer of a house removal
company. It is important that the local branch managers
are kept up to date with the law as it applies to health and
safety. He spends an hour searching the web and finds
that the best and most up-to-date information is on a UK
government site. Rather than print out the information
and post it, he e-mails all his managers telling them the
web address and asking them to read the health and safety
guidelines. So that he is confident they have read and
understood the guidelines he sends them a questionnaire
the following week that they must complete and return to
him.

These examples give a flavour of how the Internet can be used for
information and communication and, at the simplest level, for
education. They should also start you thinking about how the
Internet can be used for teaching and learning.

A brief history of the Internet

You now should have some idea of what the Internet is. You might now wonder where it all came from.

Most people think of the Internet as a very modern innovation, but its roots go back to the inventions of the nineteenth century when international communications were developed using electronic technology, such as telegraph (1836), transatlantic cable (1858–66) and the telephone (1876).

What we would probably regard as the Internet today has developed over the last 50 years. Here is a decade by decade summary of developments.

1950s

The Cold War dictated much of American military policy and the USSR's launch of Sputnik in 1957 caused the USA to respond by forming the Advanced Research Projects Agency (ARPA), a Department of Defense agency, to establish the USA's lead in military technology and science. Thus the seeds of the Internet were sown by military necessity.

1960s

A system of transferring data from computer to computer was developed because the US Air Force wanted to find a way of maintaining control over its nuclear arms in the event of nuclear attack. This system was called packet switching as the data being transferred was broken down into tiny packets of digital information. These packets could take various routes to reach their final destination so even if part of the network were destroyed, the packets could find an alternative route.

In 1969 The US Department of Defense commissioned ARPANET, which led to the development of the first network, linking four academic institutions across three states (California, Utah and Massachusetts).

1970s

The infrastructure was evolving fast. ARPANET linked 40 machines by 1972 and by 1973 it was linked to England and Norway. By the middle of the decade architecture and protocols had been developed to allow different network systems to communicate. A first commercial service was offered. The second half of the decade saw the development and growth of electronic communication with the early use of e-mail and newsgroups. Queen Elizabeth II sent an e-mail in 1976. I don't know who to.

1980s

The refining of the infrastructure continued apace as military, academic and commercial organizations worked to improve and enlarge the network. The core Internet protocol was established (known as TCP/IP) and domain names were brought into use so that complex sets of numbers no longer had to be remembered (e.g. http://www.jadu.ac.uk replaces 123.456.789.10). By the end of the decade there were more than 100 000 host computers.

1990s

This is the decade when the Internet really established itself in the public consciousness. At the beginning of the decade there were 300 000 hosts. In 1990 the first commercial service provider started business. In 1991 keyword search techniques were introduced. The European Particle Physics Laboratory in Switzerland (CERN) brought the World Wide Web into being in 1991 with the development of hypertext, and soon after a browser was developed that allowed web pages to include graphics. The term 'surfing' – hopping from link to link – was first used in 1992. The commercial potential of the Web was beginning to be recognized and in 1994 it became possible to order pizza from the Pizza Hut web site. Organizations and businesses starting using the Web as a way of widely disseminating information – Her Majesty's Treasury came online in 1994.

By the middle of the decade there were several companies providing commercial access. Compuserve was one of the first. In 1996 Microsoft had a change of mind and saw that it too must be involved (after originally rejecting the possibility that the Web would become popular). It launched the Internet Explorer browser and a browser war was declared against Netscape. By 1997 there were 19.5 million hosts and 1 million web sites. It became possible to access not only text and graphics, but sound and even video.

THE FUTURE

The Internet will increasingly use cable and fibre optic lines which will make it faster and more powerful so it will easily carry video and three-dimensional environments. It will become more secure and more and more people will have the confidence to shop on the Internet. Perhaps some sort of international currency may develop for Internet transactions. It will get bigger and yet bigger.

Web or Internet?

WWW, World Wide Web, Web, Internet, Net. Are all these terms interchangeable? No, not quite. The Web (WWW or World Wide Web) and the Internet (Net) are slightly different. The Internet incorporates all the different protocols available when computers are linked with other computers such as e-mail, newsgroups, the Web, file transfer protocol and the quaintly named gopher and archie. So the Web and e-mail are just parts of the Internet, though by far the biggest and most widely used.

Getting to know your browser

The browser is the software that you use to view web pages and it is installed on the computer you use to access the Web. It is like the window that you look through. The most widely used browsers by far are the Netscape Navigator and Microsoft Internet Explorer, so these are the ones that I have chosen to describe in detail. However, there are others available such as Opera, NCSA Mosaic and Quarterdeck WebCompass. Different browsers all have very similar features though for some reasons browser preference seems to arouse strong passions in some web users. Browser software is easy to obtain and very cheap or free.

Figure 3.1 shows the menu and toolbars of Internet Explorer version 4. And those for Netscape Navigator are shown in Figure 3.2. They are very similar so although there are small differences in

Figure 3.1   The Internet Explorer browser menu and toolbars

Figure 3.2   The Netscape Navigator browser menu and toolbars

the icons and vocabulary that each browser uses, learning how to use one will equip you to use any. Here are the main features you are likely to find on a browser.

TOOLBAR BUTTONS

- **Back** – Clicking on this button will take you back and reopen any web pages that you have visited during a session online.
- **Forward** – This button will cycle the other way and it also allows you to reopen web pages that you have visited during an online session.

  So the **Back** and **Forward** buttons are used to help you navigate back and forth revisiting pages that you have already opened during any particular session. You can also click on the tiny arrows on the back and forward buttons to get a drop down list of the last few pages you have visited.

- **Stop** – this interrupts the loading of a page, useful if it turns out to be very slow in loading perhaps because it has bandwidth heavy features such as graphics, or if you realize it is not exactly what you want, or if you change your mind.
- **Refresh/Reload** – If for any reason a web page hasn't loaded properly, clicking on this will make the browser reload that page.
- **Home** – This will take you directly to the page that has been set up in your browser as the launch page. It is the page that your browser will normally go to when you first log on. You

can choose for yourself what that page will be. My home page is the BBC News. Many people have a search tool as their home page.

- **Favourites** (Microsoft) or **Bookmarks** (Netscape) – Your browser will provide you with a way of storing web addresses of interesting and useful sites so you can revisit them without having to laboriously write down and then later retype the address. You will also be able to organize your personal list of web addresses into folders.
- **Print** – This will print the web page that you are viewing. Treat this button with caution as a web page can be very long and you may only want to print part of it.

There will be other buttons depending on the type and version of browser you use, but learning how to use these will equip you sufficiently to access the Web.

SCROLL BARS

These let you move up and down, and from side to side, if a whole web page won't fit in to a browser window. Browser scroll bars work in exactly the same way as they do in any other Windows application.

MENU BAR

Near the top of your browser is the Menu Bar. Clicking on one of the words on the Menu Bar (such as File, Edit, Help) will take you to more advanced ways of using and configuring the browser.

ADDRESS BAR

If you already know the address of the web page that you wish to visit you key it into this box and then press the Enter key on your keyboard. A web address will look something like this:

http://www.bbc.co.uk/education

MISSING TOOLBARS?

If any of these toolbars go missing, right click just to the right of the word Help on the Menu Bar. A menu will appear. Make sure Standard Buttons and Address Bar are ticked.

Web browsers are easy to use, and any learner with web access will have one. In theory a web page viewed using one browser will look more or less the same if viewed with a different browser (though this statement will be qualified in a later chapter) which means that course materials will look much the same wherever they are used. The development of the multimedia browser was therefore a gift for the online tutor.

4 FINDING YOUR WAY ROUND THE WEB

With more than 320 million pages on the Web covering almost every topic and interest you could possibly imagine (and many you probably shouldn't), the problem you and your learners will face when finding things on the Web is not 'Is it available?', but 'How on earth do I track it down?' This chapter will introduce you to the tools and strategies that you can employ to improve your chances of getting speedily to what you want.

There are three main methods of locating material on the Web. These are using:

- web addresses
- hyperlinks
- search tools.

Web addresses

Web addresses are more properly known as Uniform Resource Locators or, for short, URLs, though the term web address seems to be gaining currency. The web address is what you use if you already know the site you want. It looks something like this, though mercifully not all are quite so long:

http://www.sheffcol.ac.uk/products/prod01/key_maths.html

If you already know the web address of the site you want you can locate it by keying in the address in the box near the top of your browser screen (called the Address or Location Box), then pressing the Enter key on your keyboard. Every web page has its own individual web address, and the web address that you key in will give your browser the information it needs to locate that specific page on the web.

The construction of a web address is not quite as mysterious as it appears. Understanding how the web address above gives your browser the information that it needs can provide you with useful clues about the target web page and what you might do if your browser cannot find it.

COMPONENT PARTS

http://

This tells the browser the **protocol** used, that is the rules that govern how you wish to transfer the information. The system the Web uses is Hypertext Transfer Protocol (http).

www.sheffcol.ac.uk

This is the name of the **web server** or **domain name**. That is the computer where that particular web site (collection of web pages) is held. The uk ending tells you that the site is located in the United Kingdom. Not all web addresses have that geographic information so it is not always possible to tell in which country the web server is located. Other examples of countries are:

.de – Germany

.jp – Japan

.au – Australia

.nl – Netherlands

/products/prod01/

The computer that is hosting the web page will have some sort of file structure, similar to the hierarchical file structure on any computer. So this part of the web address shows the directory path, that is it tells the browser exactly where on that host computer the page you want is located. As you can see, the names of the directory path give some indication of the content of the web page you wish to find.

key_maths.html

This is the filename of the page you are aiming to locate – once again, the content is indicated by the name of the page. The file extension, html, stands for hypertext markup language and it is the format for all web pages.

Here are a few tips that will help you find what you want using web addresses:

1. Key in the address *exactly*, being careful to include every full stop, dash, underscore and slash – even the smallest mistake will prevent the browser finding the correct page. If your browser cannot find a page, this is the first thing you should check.
2. Web addresses *never* have spaces in them and they *never* have commas in them.
3. Web addresses *never* have the symbol @ in them (if you see an @ then it is probably an e-mail address, not a web address).
4. If you get a message saying that the web page can't be found, try deleting everything after the domain name (up to the first slash) and pressing the Enter key. This should take you to the computer hosting the page you want, and you may be able to find it from there using hyperlinks or that web site's own search facility.

Hyperlinks

On any web pages there are links which, with a single mouse click, will quickly take you either to another part of the page you are viewing, or to another page on that web site, or even to another web page on a different site altogether. The convention has been that hyperlinks were in blue and underlined, but this convention is increasingly disregarded and practically anything that appears on a web page – text, a picture or an animation – can be a link. The only sure way to tell is to move your mouse pointer around the page. If it changes to a little pointing hand then you have found a link and a single click on your left mouse button will take you to it. Once you have found your way to the web site you want it ought to be a straightforward business to navigate that web site using links.

SURFING

Surfing is hopping around the web from link to link and from site to site just following your inclination. You will find things that are amazing, amusing and appalling. Surfing is one of the joys of the web for you will find yourself becoming absorbed in reading about things that you have probably never given a moment's thought to before. For example, I have discovered whilst surfing in recent weeks: a comparison of offences committed by soldiers of various countries of the British Empire during the First World War; an essay on the altruism of eighteenth-century pirates; the effect administering various drugs has on the web-building techniques of spiders (caffeine had the worst); an article explaining how it was possible to determine the distances to nearby galaxies. Fascinating stuff and a pleasant way of passing leisure time, but it is highly unlikely that you will stumble across exactly what you are looking for by surfing.

Search tools

Search tools are sites on the Web expressly designed to help you locate exactly what you are looking for. They are essential tools for locating information and resources efficiently when you do not already know the web address. The online tutor must understand their strengths and their limitations, and learn how to use them effectively. There are lots of search tools on the Web – examples of better known ones are Yahoo, Alta Vista, HotBot and Ask Jeeves – and they all provide their services to the user free. They generate their income by carrying advertising, as is obvious when you use them.

Search tools each hold a vast database of information about the pages on the Web. Each tool collates and continually revises its database of web addresses, web page content and descriptions using automated 'robots' or 'spiders' that constantly roam the Web, returning with information to update the search tool's database. It is also possible for individuals and organizations to register their own web site with search tools to ensure that any search conducted using that tool will return their site. When you do a keyword search the search tool searches its own database and if it finds a match loads that web page for you. Thus you are not directly searching the Web itself, but the search tool's database of information.

EFFECTIVE SEARCHING

If you are going to search effectively and without wasting too much of your time then you must invest some effort in developing your search skills and strategies. The touchstones for effective searching are:

- choose the search tool appropriate to the search;
- learn the best way to use keyword searches.

You must also learn to evaluate the quality and educational value of the web sites that you find, but this skill will be left until a later chapter.

CHOOSING A SEARCH TOOL

Search tools do not all work in exactly the same way. You would be well advised to choose four or five search tools that you like, then familiarize yourself with the way each of them works and make them your first choice when you want to search.

Broadly speaking search tools work in one of two ways:

- Directories
- Keyword search tools

Directories

Yahoo is an example of a directory. On the main page of Yahoo you will find a list of categories arranged alphabetically starting with *Arts & Humanities* and ending with *Society and Culture.* Each category is further divided, then subdivided again and again. Thus under the category *Social Science* you will find about forty sub-categories (such as *Anthropology and Archaeology, Critical Theory, Economics, Linguistics, Psychology, Sociology* and *Women's Studies*). Click on *Anthropology and Archaeology* and you will find the category subdivided yet further (*Anthrozoology, Cultural Anthropology, Journals* and *Museums*) as well as a list of web sites that fall under *Anthropology and Archaeology.* You can use Yahoo by clicking your way down through the hierarchy of categories, narrowing down the field with each click, eventually leading you to the page holding the information you want.

The content of the directory's database will probably have been selected by humans – thus the database of a directory is likely to be smaller, though more pertinent, than that of a search tool that is fully automated.

Here is an example of how Yahoo might be used in doing some research.

> **Hugh's daughter** suffers from asthma and so Hugh would like to find out what he can about the condition. He goes to Yahoo's home page and clicks on *Health*, then on *Diseases and Conditions*, then on *Asthma* which takes him to links to about twenty-five different web sites about asthma including a very useful US site which provides detailed information for doctors, patients and their families.
>
> Hugh lives in London, England, so he wants to find out more about air pollution locally. He uses Yahoo again and this time takes this route through the hierarchy *Science » Ecology » Pollution » Air* and finds that University College, London, has a site about Urban Air Pollution in the UK.
>
> **Clara** is the research and development manager for an international optician group and she is attending a conference in East Europe about a new product that has been developed. She needs to find out what the local currency is, and the current exchange rate. Using Yahoo she goes though *Business & Economy » Finance & Investment » Currency* and locates Yahoo's own currency converter. She discovers that there are about 376 Hungarian Forints to a GB Pound.

Keyword search tools

Excite is an example of a search tool that uses keyword searches. These search tools offer a box where you enter the subject that you want to look up. This can be a single word, a few words or a phrase. Clicking on the Search button on the web page (*not* on the Search button on the browser tool bar) will make the search tool produce a list of likely links.

> **Clara** is off again to another international conference, this time in Pennsylvania. She already knows the currency and exchange rate, but wants to find out about opticians in the state that she could visit. She does an Excite search using the search terms *opticians Pennsylvania* and locates five local companies.

Some keyword search tools, such as Ask Jeeves, allow you to pose a question, for example 'When did Confucious die?' or 'Where can I buy malt whisky?'

Meta-search engines can be very useful. They do not have a database of their own but will search the databases of several different search tools on your behalf simultaneously. Inference Find and Metafind are both examples of this kind of search tool.

EFFECTIVE SEARCH STRATEGIES

Search engines are eager and quick, but they cannot guess what you are thinking. You must tell them precisely what you want. It is important to think carefully about the keywords that you employ so that your search does not result in an overwhelming number of suggested web sites, most of which are completely irrelevant.

Using these guidelines should help you to become an effective searcher:

- Be specific in your use of keywords. If you are interested in sticklebacks and no other fish then use **sticklebacks** as your search term rather than **fish**.
- Search tools tend to prioritize the first word in your list of keywords so think about the order in which you use them. If you are looking for red rose bushes then put the word **roses** first rather than **red** for more relevant results.
- If you are looking for a particular person, organization or title, put it in inverted commas, for example **"Indira Gandhi"** or **"African National Congress"** or **"As You Like It"**. This will return only those sites that include that particular name, organization or title.
- You can also use inverted commas to search for particular phrases such as **"solar power"** or **"cargo cults"** or **"film noir"**.
- Familiarize yourself with the way your favourite search tools work by reading their Help information.
- They may allow Boolean or Logical Operators. This means that using such words as AND, NOT and OR between keywords will help narrow down the search.
  - Use + or AND between words. Only web pages that include all the keywords you have chosen will be returned. Thus if you want to find out about museums in Italy you should use the keywords **Museums AND Italy**.

- Exclude what you don't want by using the word NOT. So if you want to find out about all soap operas except Neighbours try **"Soap Operas" AND NOT Neighbours**.
- The word OR will let the search tool bring back various alternatives. Thus if you want to know about various big cats you could search using **Lions OR Tigers OR Leopards**.

- Find out what advanced features each search tool offers. For example, Altavista allows prefixes to keywords which pin down further what you are looking for. Thus **image:cherub** finds pages with images called cherub and **title:cherub** finds pages with cherub in the title.

- Use wildcards (*) so you can search on a word with multiple endings. Thus **garden*** will find **garden, gardens, gardening, gardeners**.

- If the first search doesn't bring back useful results, then try changing the word order or use different words or phrases, or try switching to a different search tool.

- You may find it easier to use a search tool such as Ask Jeeves which allows you to ask a question such as **"Where was Nelson Mandela born?"** or **"What is the main language of Taiwan?"** Remember that these are also keyword searches and it may help to change the question slightly if the first question doesn't yield the results you want.

Here are some search strategies in action.

> **Jane** teaches Theatre Studies so wants to find out what is showing at her local theatre in Sheffield so that she can organize a class trip. She does a search using the search term **The Crucible** and finds lots of sites, but they all seem to be about Arthur Miller's play or the film of the play. She then adds **The Crucible +Sheffield** and finds plenty of sites listed, but the annual snooker championship which is held in this theatre dominates the results. Next she tries **The Crucible +Sheffield –snooker** and finds The Crucible's home page. She finds out that *The Rivals* is on and decides to do some research on the dramatist in order to produce a class handout. She does a search on **"Richard Brinsley Sheridan"** and finds exactly what she wants.
>
> **Tyrone and Jacob** are doing their maths homework and are a bit stuck with geometry. They turn to Ask Jeeves and ask **"What is Pythageerus' Theorum?"** They are

also struggling with their spelling but fortunately Ask Jeeves offers them a spellcheck facility. Not only do they find several sites which explain (with diagrams) the Pythagorean Theory, they even find a potted biography and a joke.

For the sake of clarity I have described the different types of search tools as if they all worked in a completely different way. This is not really the case and there is a considerable overlap in the way they each work. You can do a keyword search using Yahoo, and Altavista will allow you to ask a question, Excite also provides a directory.

5 USING THE INTERNET TO COMMUNICATE

For the online tutor the Internet is not only a wonderful store of information, it is the medium you will use for communication with your learners, and which your learners will use to communicate with one another. It is what makes the experience of Internet delivered education so different from traditional distance education. It may indeed be the only way you are able to communicate if your learners are geographically so far flung that the inclusion of any face-to-face interaction in your course is impractical.

There are all sorts of tools for Internet communication that will be at your disposal. These can be used in various combinations for online delivery and when designing or converting your course you need to decide which are the best ones for you to use. In this chapter we will look at the main tools that are available. These are:

● e-mail
● conferencing
● synchronous chat
● video- and audio-conferencing
● discussion lists and newsgroups.

E-mail

E-mail is simple to use, cheap, reliable and very, very quick. Why is it better than 'snail mail' (as Internet users call the old postal system)? Because you can send an e-mail to anyone in the world who has e-mail, with a few keystrokes and mouse clicks and it will be in their mailbox in seconds. No hunting around for paper, pen and envelope. No working out the cost of stamps or going to the shop to buy them. No running to the post box to catch the last post. No delays while the communication is transferred from van, to train, to plane. And all for the cost of a local telephone call.

But isn't a telephone call even quicker? Perhaps, but it costs more and international time zones mean that you may want to phone your learners at a time when they are likely to still be in bed. Or they may be out when you phone, or their phone may be engaged, or you may have to leave a message on an answerphone and not be sure if the message is decipherable.

You have time to think about what you want to say too.

Once you start using e-mail you will wonder how you ever managed without it.

One cautionary note. E-mail is so quick and easy to send, and to forward to others that it should not be regarded as quite as private as a letter. So don't say anything in e-mail that is libellous or inflammatory. Be as cautious as you would be when sending a postcard.

E-MAIL SOFTWARE

There are various e-mail software packages, for example Outlook Express which comes bundled with Microsoft Internet Explorer, or Netscape Mail which comes with Netscape Navigator. There is also 'dedicated' e-mail software such as Pegasus or Eudora. This sort of e-mail is all loaded on to your computer's hard disk and can usually be used off-line, that is you can read and reply to messages, and organize your messages without being connected to the Internet, thus saving money on connection costs.

Another type of e-mail is the web-based 'free' e-mail. These are e-mail services provided by companies that do not charge, but make their money by carrying advertisements. Hotmail, Yahoo Mail and Talk21 are examples of these. Normally all you have to do is fill in an online form and agree to their conditions. The main disadvantage of these is that you will probably have to be online to use them – this can prove expensive and is often slower than working off-line. However, it may be a good idea to set yourself up with a web e-mail account as you can access it from any computer in the world that is connected to the Internet; you don't have to be sitting at your usual machine.

Both you and your learners will need to have access to e-mail, but it doesn't matter if their e-mail system is different to yours. An e-mail sent from, say, a Hotmail account will be readable in Outlook Express.

FEATURES OF E-MAIL

Whichever e-mail system you use, they will all provide certain basic features, as discussed below.

Composing messages

When you want to compose a message you will be presented with a box which will look something like that shown in Figure 5.1.

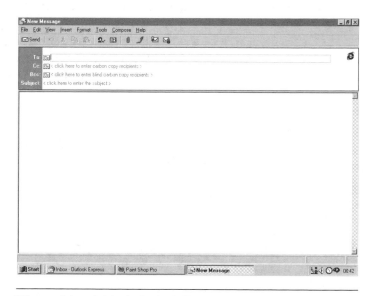

Figure 5.1   A blank Outlook Express e-mail message window

The first thing you need to do is enter the e-mail address of the person you are sending to in the **To:** box. An e-mail address will look something like this:

anne.dunmore@asn.ac.uk

The @ in the address tells you that this is an e-mail address (URLs or web addresses never have an @ in the address, e-mails always do).

If you want to send the same e-mail to several people at once you can put all their e-mail addresses in the **To:** box with a comma between each e-mail address, thus:

anne.dunmore@asn.ac.uk, w.gromit@talk21.com, orwell@global.net.

If you want to send a copy of an e-mail to anyone, their e-mail address goes into the **Cc:** box. Again you can put several addresses here, separated by commas.

The **Bcc:** stands for Blind Carbon Copy. If you want to copy your e-mail to someone without the main recipient knowing, then put their e-mail address in this box.

In the **Subject:** box give the e-mail a message title that is short, but gives the recipient(s) some idea of the content. Avoid vague subjects such as *Greetings*, *Assignment* and *From Me*. Not only will recipients want to have an idea of what the subject is before they read it, they may also want to find it again in the future once it has been stored, and a brief and clear subject will facilitate that.

Finally type in your message. Later in this chapter I will consider in more detail the conventions and etiquette of e-mail but at this point all I shall say is keep it to the point, and don't feel you have to be as formal as if you were writing a letter.

So your completed e-mail might look something like the example given in Figure 5.2.

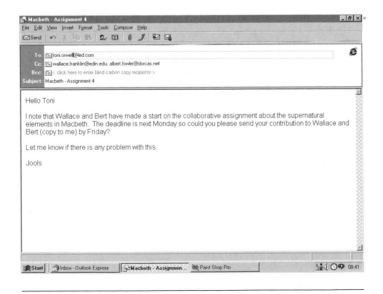

Figure 5.2   A completed e-mail message

All you have to do then is click on the **Send** button. This may send the e-mail directly, or it may deposit it into your personal electronic out-box so that next time you connect to the Internet all your e-mails will be sent in one batch (and you will be able to download all the e-mails that have been sent to you since you last connected).

In-box

Your e-mail will have an in-box. When you connect to the Internet to collect e-mails that have been sent to you, this is where they will appear. You will see a list of all your new e-mails, and the in-box will probably also tell you who each is from, the subject, and the date and time it was sent. There will also be some indication that they are as yet unread – a little flag may appear beside them, or they may be in bold. Once opened and read the indicator will disappear. Urgent e-mails may also be indicated in some way, perhaps with an exclamation mark.

It is good practice to deal with each e-mail as you read it and move it out of your in-box. Some may be irrelevant and can be deleted immediately. Some you may want to store for future reference. Some you will reply to immediately. Some you may want to forward to someone else. Some may need a considered response that will take a few days so you should just acknowledge them and store them till you can respond properly.

Your in-box will have a reply button. Clicking on this while you have an e-mail selected, or while it is open, will generate a window like the Compose message window, only it will already have some boxes filled: In the **To:** box will be the e-mail address of the sender of the message, in the **Subject:** box will be the subject with Re: in front of it, and the original message may appear too. You can either delete the original message, or add your message above, below or interleaved, as shown in Figure 5.3. There should also be a facility that allows you to reply to any other people that the original e-mail was sent to, as well as the sender.

Folders

You will be able to create and name your own folders and sub-folders to store e-mails that you receive. Your online tutoring will not be successful if you are not well organized, and that should start with your e-mail system. You will need a folder for each course you teach online. This needs to be divided into sub-folders, certainly a folder for each learner and perhaps folders for particular units or sections of

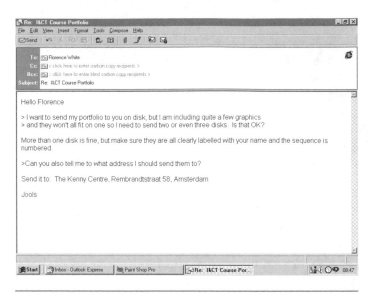

Figure 5.3   A reply to an e-mail message

your course, or for each assignment or exercise. How these sub-folders are organized will depend on you and the course that you teach but, believe me, don't think you will be able to properly manage your course if you leave all your e-mails in an ever-extending in-box!

Address book
Another invaluable facility. In order to save you time painstakingly keying in e-mail addresses every time you send an e-mail, you can store commonly used e-mail addresses (and probably other contact information) in an address book. Your address book will also allow you to create your own 'Groups'. For example, you may often want to send the same e-mail to all the other course tutors who teach the same course as you, or to all the learners in a particular tutorial group. You should therefore create and name a group, then when you put the name of that e-mail group in the **To:** box the message will be sent to everyone in that group.

Sending attachments
E-mail is normally plain text, but as a tutor you may wish to send and receive word-processed documents, graphics, spreadsheets, web pages or even programs. This is possible with e-mail by sending such files as attachments. After composing your e-mail click on whatever icon, button or menu brings up the attachment dialogue box. Choose the file (or files) you wish to attach. Then when you send that e-mail the recipient will also receive the attachment.

There are considerable benefits to this:

- More complex formatting features can be used than are available in plain e-mail, such as coloured fonts, tables or columns.
- The files sent are editable by the recipient, for example the figures in a spreadsheet can be modified, corrected or updated.
- Tutors can utilize word-processing features to give feedback on assignments received, such as adding comments.
- Learners can work collaboratively to compile a document or create a piece of work.

But beware! There are a few dangers associated with sending attachments:

- Attachments (unlike plain text e-mail) can carry computer viruses so you and your learners will need to own and use up-to-date anti-virus software.
- Files need to be in a 'portable' format. For example, a document saved in one word-processing format (say Wordperfect) may not be readable in a different format (say Wordpro). Portable formats are formats that ought to be readable by many programmes. Examples of these are Rich Text Format (RTF), which can be produced and read in any word processor, or Joint Photographic Experts Group (JPEG), which can be read by almost any graphics package.
- Some attachments, particularly graphics, are large and can use up valuable bandwidth and be slow when sending and receiving.

But don't be completely put off by these warnings – the ability to send attachments is invaluable, but make sure early in the course that you can exchange attachments in a readable form with all of your learners.

Conferencing

Although e-mail provides interactive opportunities between tutor and learner, and learner and learner, conferencing will add yet a further dimension to the opportunity for collaborative work and conversations in an online course. Conferencing can be synchronous or asynchronous, it can be just plain text or enhanced with such things as graphics or hyperlinks, it can include audio and video.

TEXT CONFERENCING SYSTEMS

The broad distinction between e-mail and conferencing is that e-mail travels from one person to another person, or a group of people, and then goes into each individual's mailbox. Each individual then decides how to deal with that e-mail – reply to it, delete it or move it to one of the folders that they have created. A conference system, on the other hand, is structured and managed by the tutor, and learners will have to log-on to their course conference in order to read and respond to messages.

The screen shot of a conference in Figure 5.4 shows a typical conferencing interface. This is a WebBoard conference and different conferences will have somewhat different interfaces, features and vocabulary, and may be web-based or may need the learners to install software on to their own computers. However, any conferencing system will allow the tutor to set up sub-conferences which reflect how that tutor wants group discussion/conversations and collaborative work to be organized. For example, a tutor might set up a mix of sub-conferences for each module of the course, for each learning set or small group, for tutor announcements, for social interactions, for technical questions and answers. The tutor should be able to control who has password access to the conference, and in some cases to each sub-conference.

Learners can send messages to any of these conferences by replying to a previous message or by starting a new thread (topic). Thus in the example screen shot we can see that the tutor, Jools Duggleby, has created four conferences: *Coffee Bar, Creating a web site,*

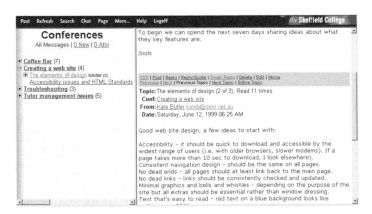

Figure 5.4   The WebBoard conferencing system

Troubleshooting and *Tutor management issues*. Clicking on the symbol to the left of the *Creating a web site* conference has displayed a list of the topics, clicking on the symbol to the left of the topic title displays a list of messages, clicking on the message will display that message in the right-hand screen. As the course progresses conferences can be added, and conferences that are obsolete can be deleted.

When learners access the conference it should be clear to them what the conferences are, what topics are being discussed within each conference, who has posted to each conference, the date of each posting, and which postings they have not yet read.

The tutor has the power to edit and manipulate the messages too. This may be necessary if a learner sends a message to the wrong conference and it needs to be moved, or if the message has gone off-topic and needs a new subject heading. Occasionally a tutor may feel that a message is likely to damage group coherence in some way, for example because it is offensive, and so will wish to delete it. The tutor's role in managing conferences will be explored more fully in Chapter 11.

Other features that should be available in a conferencing system are:

● search and filter tools so that learners can easily locate topics and text within messages;
● a facility for users to provide mini-biographies.

FREE CONFERENCING

To get a good conferencing system you will have to pay for it and naturally the better the system, the more you will have to pay. But there are free conferencing services on the Web which you could utilize. You can set them up for free and, as the 'owner', decide who can join and who cannot. They will provide as a minimum some sort of message posting system, and may provide additional services such as a calendar and a chat room. They do offer a reasonable alternative for anyone who would like to incorporate conferencing but has limited financial resources.

Synchronous chat

Increasingly conferencing systems include the facility for

synchronous chat. This enables people who are logged on to the conference simultaneously to have a conversation in real time by typing a message in a box and clicking on send. The message then can be read by the other person or persons in the chatroom. In theory it is possible for tutor and learner or learner and learner to have a tutorial or a discussion about an idea or collaborate on a task. However, tutors and learners may find chat rather a disappointing education tool for the following reasons:

- The ebb and flow of conversation is slowed by the keyboarding speed of each participant.
- Conversational points tend to overlap, thus making a discussion difficult to follow.
- If there are several people in the chatroom then the problem of conversation overlap is magnified, so strict rules about taking turns have to be agreed and adhered to.
- There is a pressure to respond quickly, so contributions tend to be short.
- There is little time to give thought to the content and shaping of contributions.

Video-conferencing

Like chat, video-conferencing takes place in real time. It works because all who access it will use a camera (often a very tiny one sitting on top of a monitor) and a microphone. Both video and audio are carried across the Internet instantly and so conversation takes place where faces can be seen, body language read and voices heard. It most closely replicates the experience of face-to-face learning.

The potential of video-conferencing for teaching and learning online is immense since it is possible to recreate both the formal atmosphere of the lecture room and the informal atmosphere of a small group discussion. It allows tutors to give demonstrations when teaching such practical subjects as cake decorating or bricklaying, and will allow learners to demonstrate that they have acquired those skills. Skills where the use of spoken language is important can be more easily taught, for example counselling, customer care or a foreign language. It is possible to show diagrams or drawings or play back a relevant pre-recorded video, and to invite an expert guest lecturer to speak.

The main problem with video-conferencing is that further technological development is needed before it can be introduced routinely into online courses. There is no single protocol that allows different systems to communicate with each other; quality can be variable with lip movements being out of synchronization with what is being spoken and both video and, more importantly, audio quality is variable; high quality systems are expensive and out of the reach of the budgets of many organizations, let alone learners.

Audio-conferencing

Audio-conferencing uses the phone to connect two or more people together for synchronous discussion. Although large numbers of people can be connected together, audio-conferencing is only practical as a means of communication between a smaller number of people. Its main advantage is its simplicity since anyone can use a telephone. It also has economic advantages over video-conferencing. It depends, of course, on all participants being available at the same time.

Discussion lists and newsgroups

You should be aware of the existence of discussion lists and newsgroups which are both commonly used for group communications on the Internet.

DISCUSSION LISTS

Discussion lists are communities of people who share an interest and use ordinary e-mail to discuss it. Thus if you were particularly interested in meteorology you could subscribe to a meteorology discussion list. Every message sent to the list is 'bounced' to all the other subscribers, including any message you send. As is usually the case on the Internet there is a discussion list for practically every topic you can think of. To give you a flavour there are currently lists discussing dachshunds, clean jokes, silent movies and typography. To find out what discussion lists are available, a good starting point is a free web service called Liszt (www.liszt.com) which helps you find and subscribe to existing lists. As I write Liszt has a directory of more than 90 000 discussion lists. Not every list is open to all – there may be some sort of moderator who 'gatekeeps', that is decides whether you are eligible to subscribe. It is also possible to start your own discussion list, though this is not usually a free service.

NEWSGROUPS

Newsgroups are also a communications method for people who share a common interest. Again there is a newsgroup for almost any interest. You will need some sort of newsgroup reading program (a newsreader) to access them. This software can usually be obtained for free, and comes bundled with Internet Explorer and Netscape Navigator. Your Internet Service Provider will carry a list of the newsgroups to which it will give you access.

Newsgroups work like a bulletin board. Within the broad interest of that particular group there will be messages on various sub-topics (threads). It is possible to follow a discussion on a particular topic by reading through each message on that thread. You can also post your own messages, and start new threads.

Netiquette

Netiquette is a neologism that expresses the idea that there is a right and a wrong way to behave when communicating on the Internet. This has led to some people feeling inhibited in their online behaviour, but there is little to fear. In most cases common sense and courtesy will ensure that conduct online will not cause any offence.

In any online course it should be made clear to learners what behaviour is expected of them, both generally in online interactions and specifically for your course. It might well be that online behaviour makes a good subject for a conference early on in the course, or you might prefer to predetermine what is acceptable. Make sure that your learners know the rules and are aware of the consequences of flouting them.

Here are some general guidelines for acceptable behaviour when communicating via the Internet:

1. Remember that the people with whom you are communicating have feelings – treat them with same politeness and respect

that you would in any other social situation.

2. Be sensitive to the fact that other cultures may have different manners to your own and that these will manifest themselves online.

3. Respect people's time – don't send long-winded e-mails or send e-mails unnecessarily.

4. Respect people's bandwidth – don't send very large attachments without their prior knowledge and agreement.

5. Respect people's privacy – don't forward private e-mails without their permission.

6. Proofread your communications to check grammar, spelling and sense.

7. Don't provoke angry arguments or be drawn into the arguments of others (this is called 'flaming' on the Internet) – by all means disagree with others, but do so politely.

8. Be tolerant of other people, especially those new to the Internet.

9. Be generous and share the knowledge that you have.

10. Don't type exclusively in capital letters – it is considered bad form on the Internet.

SMILEYS AND ABBREVIATIONS

Smileys were developed as an aid to smooth communications on the Internet, the idea being that in the absence of body language and intonation something else was needed to convey emotion. It seems to me that as the use of the Internet widens, smileys are decreasing in use, but here are a few that you may encounter or wish to use:

:-(Sadness

:-) A smile

;-) A wink

I am not keen on smileys personally, but if you are making a comment and you are unsure of how it may be received a smiley should ensure that what you have said is taken in the right spirit.

A collection of abbreviations has been developed to save on keystrokes when typing messages. Here are a few examples of these:

BTW – By the way

FYI – For your information

IMO – In my opinion

Only use smileys and these kinds of abbreviations if you are absolutely sure all the recipients of your message are familiar with them. Remember, the aim is to communicate politely, clearly and unambiguously, not to mystify with esoteric symbols!

Which methods of communications should you choose?

The communication tools you use for your course will depend upon what you are trying to achieve, and what your budget can stand. You will most certainly use e-mail, which is the core communications tool on the Internet. If you want to include some interaction within your learner group you will need more: a discussion list, a newsgroup or some sort of conferencing system. Video-conferencing can be built in only if you are certain that your learners will have access to it, and that their system is compatible with yours.

If we consider the interactions in a face-to-face course then their equivalent in an online course might look like this:

Face to face	*Online*
Conversation between tutor and learner (for example clarifying a point, monitoring progress, giving feedback on assignments)	One-to-one e-mail
Conversation between learner and learner (such as discussion about an assignment, social exchange)	One-to-one e-mail
Non-tutor led discussion between group of learners (such as small group work on particular task)	Group e-mail, conference, discussion list/conference
Lecture by tutor	Web-based materials or conference
Tutor-led discussion (such as small or whole group exploration of an issue)	Conference
Social conversation (such as chatting in a canteen)	Group e-mail or conference which can be open to all or private

PART *III*

The planning cycle

6 PLANNING THE COURSE

By now this book should have persuaded you that there is a growing market for online courses, and that the technology exists and is sufficiently widespread to make it a viable option for providers. What is more it seems highly likely that online learning will prove a popular way of learning. It may well be that the course you wish to teach already exists, but needs to be converted for online delivery. Or it may be that you wish to design a new course from scratch specifically for delivery online. What you must think about now is the process that needs to be undertaken in order to get a course ready to roll out to learners.

Preliminary preparation and research

The first thing you need to do is to spend time doing some preparation and research:

- Find out if you or your organization have the necessary technological and support systems in place to deliver the course, or if your organization is willing to develop them.
- Find out if you or your organization have the necessary time and money to invest in developing an online course.

And if the answer is yes, then:

- Equip yourself with the basic skills you are going to need on the Internet, particularly searching skills and e-mail use.
- Learn the fundamentals of good web page and site design.
- Examine other comparable online courses and learn from their example. Consider what you want to emulate and what you want to avoid.
- Search on the Internet for web sites that will enable you to inform yourself about the principles and practice of online education.

- Make contact with other practitioners by subscribing to relevant discussion lists and newsgroups. You will be impressed by the Internet community's willingness to share with you its experience and expertise.
- Do some market research to find out if there will be enough people who wish to enrol on your online course to make its development viable.

What can be taught online?

Be imaginative. Don't feel that because a course is being delivered at a distance that it imposes severe restraint on what can be taught. Here are some examples of courses that are currently being taught over the Internet, which should give you a flavour of what can be done:

- Dynamic Systems and Controls Laboratory
- Investments Analysis
- Introduction to World Music
- Scope of Gerontological Nursing
- Construction Materials
- Travellers' Japanese
- Introduction to Classical Islamic Civilization
- Studying the Universe with Space Observations
- History of the Vikings
- The Eighteenth-Century Novel: Narrative Contention

Work on the assumption that what you wish to deliver can be taught online, though accept that there may be some elements in any course that present a significant challenge. Examples of these could be:

- courses where oracy is tested (foreign languages);
- courses that require access to expensive equipment;
- courses involving a significant amount of practical skill development (scuba diving);
- courses where unsupervised instruction could pose a danger to the learner or to others (driving a car);
- courses aimed at learners with low literacy levels.

Think about:

- What theoretical underpinning needs to be taught?

- How can practical skills be taught and practised?
- Does the online course need supplementing with other materials such as video?

Learning outcomes and assessment criteria

If you are designing a course from scratch then the first stage in course design is determining its overall intentions. Simply put, this is

- deciding what you want the learners to acquire in terms of skills, knowledge and qualities;
- deciding the methods you will employ to measure when those skills, knowledge and qualities have been acquired.

Once these learning outcomes and assessment criteria are in place you have the start and end points for your course. What will follow in the planning cycle is determining the course content necessary to ensure that those learning outcomes and assessment criteria are achieved.

WRITING LEARNING OUTCOMES

Start by writing down a few statements about what the learning outcomes of the course are in terms of what skills, knowledge and experience you wish your learners to have gained by the end of the course.

Here are some examples of the process that two tutors might go through when designing their courses.

> **Paula** is a teacher and a practising artist who has been asked to design an art appreciation course for online delivery to learners who have no prior experience of art appreciation. She feels that it is important that learners learn something about the context of art, what art forms exist and how individuals can respond to art. After some thought and some discussion with colleagues these are the learning outcomes she feels are right for her course:
>
> Learners will:

1. Understand what art is.
2. Be aware of various art forms.
3. Know that historical and cultural factors influence art.
4. Develop a personal aesthetic value.

George works for a company providing professional development training. He is asked by a local authority to devise a course that will enable care workers in children's homes to understand better how a child develops. These are the learning outcomes which the care workers need to aim for:

1. Understand the basis of child development.
2. Understand the social and psychological influences on children.
3. Recognize how social and emotional development is affected.
4. Recognize how care workers can help a child's development.

When you write learning outcomes you should do so in a way that ensures that both you and potential learners are aware of what areas of learning will be covered by the course that is being offered. They need to be general statements of intent.

WRITING ASSESSMENT CRITERIA

This is the next stage in course design. You will need to decide what the learners must demonstrate in order for you, and them, to be sure that they have achieved the learning outcomes. Thus for each learning outcome you need to write down one or more statements about what your learners will be able to do at the end of the course. These statements must be written so that it is clear what the learner must 'produce' – something that is tangible and measurable and can be judged objectively. These are some learning outcomes that Paula and George might propose.

Paula needs now to write down what her learners will need to do to convince her that they appreciate art. Here are some assessment criteria that might be useful for her course:

Learning Outcome 3: Know that historical and cultural factors influence art

Assessment Criteria: The learner will:

1. Produce a time line that shows the significant artistic movements of a selected country, for example France.
2. Produce a study of an artist that explores and evaluates the impact of historical and cultural influences on his/her work.

George decides that these are the assessment criteria that will demonstrate that the childcare workers 'Recognize how social and emotional development is affected':

The worker will:

1. Maintain an observational diary that records the behaviour of one child over two months.
2. Describe how various factors have worked to influence the child's behaviour.

Look at the example of a completed grid used in the design of an online course delivering Internet skills (Figure 6.1). Such a grid may be a useful way to structure learning outcomes and assessment criteria. See Appendix C for a blank grid.

Different forms of online courses

The next stage of course design is to consider alternatives for structuring the delivery of the course. Questions that you could be asking yourself are:

1. Should this course be delivered exclusively online, or will it need face-to-face sessions?
2. Will the course be supplemented with non-Internet course materials such as books, hardcopy worksheets and handouts, video, audio?
3. Will the learners work individually, or will pair or group work be incorporated?
4. Will the learners work entirely at their own pace, or will they have to meet deadlines?

Let's consider what you need to take into account when considering these questions.

the **SHEFFIELD COLLEGE**

Unit Specification

Title

INFORMATION RETRIEVAL ON THE WWW: GETTING CONFIDENT

Learning outcomes

Number	Details	Number	Details
1	Efficiently navigate the WWW	3	Use basic search techniques
2	Process retrieved information locally	4	Present retrieved information

Assessment criteria – The learner will:

Number	Details	Number	Details
1.1	Utilize menus, hotlinks and other features of web pages	3.1	Choose an appropriate search engine
1.2	Make effective use of bookmarks	3.2	Use appropriate methods to refine a search
1.3	Make effective use of features of browser	3.3	Save the results of searches
2.1	Cut material from web pages and paste locally	3.4	Assess the appropriateness of information sources located
2.2	Save and print locally	4.1	Create a report making suitable use of a variety of web sources
2.3	Save files locally		

Figure 6.1 Learning outcomes and assessment criteria grid: Internet skills course

SHOULD THE COURSE BE DELIVERED EXCLUSIVELY ONLINE?

This decision depends on the target group and the subject matter of the course.

There are certainly benefits in including a face-to-face session in an online course. An initial session may be useful to introduce learners to any new technology that is being used on the course. Administrative jobs such as enrolment can be done on the spot. It may help with learner confidence and motivation if they meet the tutor and their fellow learners. Questions and answers can be dealt with immediately, thus saving valuable time once the course is in progress. Intermediate and course-end face-to-face sessions may give good opportunities for reinforcing the group work, sharing experiences or course evaluation. Skills that are difficult to teach and practise online can be covered at a face-to-face session. However, online courses are very likely to have learners who, for example, lead busy lives or are geographically widespread. Will they all be able to attend? If not, what are the implications for those who cannot?

DOES THE COURSE NEED SUPPLEMENTARY COURSE MATERIALS?

There are no hard and fast rules but again the target group and subject matters are factors to be taken into account. If your course has to use video to any extent then it will be quicker, cheaper and more reliable to send your learners pre-recorded tapes rather than attempt to mount video on the Internet. For the time being there are too many technological and bandwidth challenges. For audio materials some of the same reservations apply, though sound is less demanding technologically and does not consume bandwidth to the same extent. Pictures and text are probably easiest to mount on your course web site, rather than send via snail mail.

WILL LEARNERS WORK INDIVIDUALLY?

One of the crucial differences between traditional distance education and online delivery is the opportunities online delivery provides for incorporating communication between learners. This difference should be fully exploited by the online tutor.

As a minimum, social interaction between learners should be

encouraged. Learners should be aware of the names and e-mail addresses of other course participants and should be encouraged to get to know one another by exchanging some personal information. If the course group is very large, learners could be formed into learning sets of three to six people, perhaps based on common interests or ability. If a conferencing system is used, conferences can be set up that are specifically used for social contacts. These conferences can be given such names as 'Rest and Recreation' or 'The Virtual Pub' that encourage your learners to use the conference for social chat, telling of jokes, gossip, etc. Just the sort of things they might talk about outside of the classroom.

It is also possible and highly desirable to incorporate group work in an online course. Such groups could be established at the start of a course and work together throughout the whole course, or groups can be formed and reformed throughout the course so that different people work together at different times.

What is the right size for such groups? Between three and six people seems about right. Working in pairs is a risk because if one person drops out of the course, either permanently or temporarily, the other half of the pair is left without anyone to work with. More than six means that collaborative work can become too unwieldy.

Group work not only means that learners don't work in isolation, it also means that they have the opportunity to learn from one another through discussion, argument and exchange of experiences and skills. Group members can give one another support too. This can be practical advice about resolving technical issues, advice about locating useful information, or providing a sympathetic shoulder to cry on. It also encourages learners to keep pace with the rest of the learners if they feel that being slow will hold up the other members of their group.

Of course, not all learners like to work in groups and some specifically choose distance education because they do not want any social interactions. If you decide that group work is an essential element in the course you design, then you must make it absolutely clear to all potential learners that that is the case.

Later in the book we will look at various collaborative activities that can be included in an online course.

WILL THE LEARNERS WORK ENTIRELY AT THEIR OWN PACE, OR WILL THEY HAVE TO MEET DEADLINES?

For many learners the flexibility offered by distance education is what makes it attractive to them. They can fit their course workload around other demands on their time from work or families. They can work intensively for periods and take time off when it suits them. However, by incorporating this degree of flexibility in the pacing of the course you may also be creating some problems.

- Learners may find the lack of enforced deadlines demotivating and allow themselves to drift for a while then grind to a halt.
- Pair and group work is difficult to organize because students' progress through the course isn't synchronized.
- It is difficult to plan your own workload coherently if you have no idea when you will be receiving work from your learners, or over how long a period.
- This will have institutional implications in that resourcing and fees policy becomes problematic.

It may be possible to find a balance that will give learners some, but not absolute, flexibility.

If the course you are planning has no element of cooperative work then it is easier for learners to work at their own pace. But think about how that is to be managed within your organization:

- How many learners will you be allocated at a time?
- If learners can join the course at any time, what is the maximum number of learners a tutor can be expected to look after?
- How is it to be determined whether these learners are still 'active', though temporarily quiet?
- Will the learner stay enrolled on the course indefinitely for the single course fee?

If the course is to involve collaboration between learners then ask the following questions:

- Do the learners need to be at the same point in the course in order to collaborate effectively or will different paces slow down faster learners?
- Can collaborative groups be formed and reformed according to the point the learner has reached in the course?

- Could time markers be included in the course so that learners can control roughly the pace of the work, provided they all start particular sections at the same time?
- What will your response be as a tutor if a marker is missed?
- What do you do about learners who insist on racing ahead of your time schedule?

7 THE CONTENT OF YOUR COURSE

Building on the framework

Once you have decided upon your course's learning outcomes and assessment criteria, you then have the framework for your course. This chapter will help you build on that framework and fully develop an online course by considering the various elements that can be incorporated. Additionally, this chapter will explore the possibilities for online course content, raise some issues for you to ponder, and help you make decisions about the content of your course. As a starting point look at examples of the elements of a face-to-face course and see what their online equivalent could be.

Face to face	*Online*
Lectures	Materials mounted on to a web site
Handouts	Materials mounted on to a web site or sent as attachments to e-mails
Audio-visual aids	Graphics, animations, sound and video files
Additional readings	Links to other relevant web sites
Learner activities	Learner activities using a variety of online methods
Research using a library	Research using the Web
Written assignments	Assignments sent via e-mail

cont'd

Face to face	Online
Practical work	Various, depending on nature of practical work
Whole group discussion	Group conferencing using a conferencing system
Small group discussion	Sub-conferencing using a conferencing system
Tutorials	E-mails between learner and tutor
Assessment	Assessment using a variety of online methods

Do *not* make the mistake of simply rewriting your lecture notes into web pages as this is a dreadful waste of the medium. You will need to think about how the web site will be broken down into individual pages; how the navigation of the web site will work; what the site will look like; what interactivity can be incorporated; how the site can be enhanced with multimedia; what activities the learners will do and how their work will be assessed; and how the course participants can develop a group identity. The next chapter will consider some of the more technical aspects of web design; this chapter will focus on the content from a pedagogical point of view.

Lectures and handouts

In any course there is a core of knowledge that needs to be passed from the tutor to the learner. This core of knowledge will include such things as factual content, theory, methodology, issues and specialized vocabulary and concepts. This is an example from an Introduction to Social Science module:

Generic core	Social science examples
Factual content	Definitions of social science Scientific method Subdivisions of social science: sociology, psychology, economics, anthropology
Theory	The history of social science Introduction to its developers: Marx, Mead, Keynes Contemporary theorists
Methodology	Research methods: case studies, surveys, observation Data analysis
Issues	Objectivity Cultural bias Conflicting theories
Specialized vocabulary and concepts	Society, stratification, norm, gender

In an ordinary classroom this knowledge is frequently transferred to the learners by the tutor, who will stand at the front giving information and explanations, writing and drawing on a board, doing demonstrations and giving out handouts. Thus one of the tasks in developing an online course is to identify what this core of knowledge is, and record and organize it so that it can be mounted on course web pages. Think about the following areas.

ORDER

You will need to organize the information into units/sections/ modules with headings and sub-headings. Additionally, you will have to identify points where the learners need to participate in activities that will allow you to check that they are progressing through the course and are understanding the content.

CLARITY

When you write your materials make sure that what you say is absolutely clear. You will not be able to use any intonation, emphasis or gesture that will help your learners interpret what you say so you must be confident that what you are writing is completely unambiguous.

EXPLANATIONS

In a face-to-face classroom learners can immediately seek clarification, explanation and expansion if they do not understand what the tutor has said. In an online course learners can ask for additional information using e-mail, but this process inevitably takes longer than in a classroom so make sure that all the information a learner is likely to need is included.

LANGUAGE LEVEL

Think about the language you use and make sure it is appropriate to your target learners. Adopt a tone that is friendly and readable but avoids being patronizing.

SPECIALIST LANGUAGE

If you need to use specialist terms then explain them the first time they are used, or turn them into hyperlinks which, when clicked on, will take the learner to a glossary. Avoid jargon.

HANDOUTS

Can the handouts you usually pass round be incorporated into the material? If you wish to retain them as handouts then they can be e-mailed or mounted on the web as word-processing documents, then downloaded and printed out by the learner.

Before you start worrying about any web authoring invite someone to read through what you have written and give you feedback on its clarity and comprehensiveness.

Multimedia

GRAPHICS

Attractive graphics can easily be incorporated into your web site, be they photographs, drawings or diagrams. They can be scanned in, or created on a computer then saved in a commonly used web format, and then included in the web design. Incorporating web graphics will impact on the speed with which your web page loads so include them only if they are necessary to enhance and illustrate the learning, to assist site navigation or to provide your site with a coherent look. Do not use them merely for decoration or because your web author wants to show off his or her design skills. Too many graphics and your web page will just look a mess.

SOUND

Sound can also be recorded and uploaded, but downloading sound files will take time and in order to play them back your learners will need a multimedia computer and the appropriate software. Such software is usually easy and cheap (or free) to obtain. Remember that in many public access points such as learning centres and libraries sound is disabled so as not to disturb other users, though headphones may be made available. Can you be certain that all your students will be able to hear sound? For certain courses sound files may be invaluable, even essential – courses on music or modern foreign languages spring to mind – but as with graphics let educational necessity be the criterion for including them.

VIDEO

Video and animations can also be included and the same caution that applies when deciding whether or not to use sound must also apply, only more so. Video takes even longer than sound to download.

I apologize if I appear to be over-cautious about the incorporation of multimedia elements. Internet delivery opens up tremendous possibilities for exciting and interactive course materials that could not easily be incorporated into either distance or face-to-face education. Of course, you should use them if they enhance the course. But educational validity should be the only test for inclusion.

Additional reading

The opportunity to build in links to other sources of information on the Web is one of the most valuable gains that an online course has over both traditional distance and face-to-face courses. At the fingertips (literally) of your learners is an ever open and gigantic library that you can help them explore. As in a face to face course much of the learning consists of students reading either required or optional texts or undertaking independent research. The next chapter will point you in some useful directions and help you make judgements about the sites to which your course can usefully link and the independent research tasks that you might propose for your learners.

Learner activities

LEARNING STYLES

Not all learners learn in the same way: some like to learn some theory first, others like to launch straight in and have a go; some prefer to learn from written text, others like to see photographs and diagrams; some want to work things out by themselves, others want to develop their ideas and understanding through discussion with other learners; some like to pace their work evenly, others are happier with a last minute pre-deadline flurry; some feel that continuous assessment is the best way for them to show what they can do, others want an end of course examination. For learners there is no right or wrong way to learn – if they are learning then what they are doing is right for them. It is up to you to ensure that their course content encompasses a range of varied activities that will meet the learning needs of all learners. David Kolb developed a Learning Style Inventory that categorized different learners and their styles thus:

- Converger – prefers to tackle complex technical tasks and problems.
- Diverger – prefers to observe, think and discuss before taking action.
- Assimilator – prefers exploring abstract ideas, theories and concepts.
- Accommodator – prefers to be hands-on.

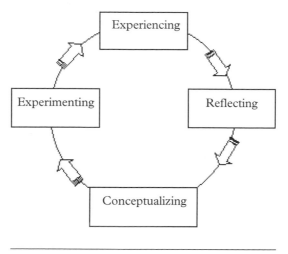

Figure 7.1   Kolb's learning cycle

LEARNING CYCLE

There are a variety of theoretical models of the learning cycle to read about. To find out more try doing searches on such exponents as Kolb, Honey and Mumford, Felder, and Silverman. Figure 7.1 is based on the Kolb model.

Since the Kolb model is a cyclical rather than a linear model there is no 'first stage'. The learner goes through the cycle repeatedly but doesn't re-enter a stage at the same level each time, rather the learner will repeat the cycle each time at a higher or more complex level or with a greater degree of confidence and independence. Learning will occur as the learner progresses through each stage of the learning cycle. Thus a course would need to ensure that a learner tries something out (concrete experience), considers the experience (reflective observation), synthesizes the experience and the reflection to form a conclusion (abstract conceptualization), and then tests this learning in new circumstances (active experimentation).

Here is an example of a series of activities from a course for careers guidance workers which allows learners to progress through the learning cycle.

Concrete experience

Joan, a trainee careers guidance worker, conducts a taped

face-to-face interview with a new client and then makes a written record of the interview.

Reflective observation

The transcript of the interview is circulated to a small group of other learners on Joan's course (her learning set) and the tutor via e-mail, who give e-mail feedback on the questions and other interventions that Joan used during her interview. Joan also has the opportunity to read other learners' transcripts.

The tutor suggests Joan and her learning set look at some specified web sites on verbal communication.

Abstract conceptualization

Joan writes a report on the strengths and weaknesses of the interview she conducted and circulates this to her learning set.

Her learning set together produces a checklist stating what points need to be covered and what pitfalls should be avoided in a first career interview. This checklist is posted to the course online conference as a reference document for the whole course group.

Active experimentation

Joan conducts another interview using the checklist for reference.

Thus you must embed activities into your course that ensure learners progress logically through the learning cycle and provide a mix that will suit each individual's learning style. The details of these activities need to be subject specific of course, but here are some suggestions that might help you with ideas for your course activities.

RESEARCH

Expect your learners to do some exploration themselves. A vital study skill that online learners must possess is the ability to locate relevant web sites and make judgements about how valuable those sites will be to their learning. As a starting point you could simply ask learners to locate useful sites and e-mail the web addresses to you. As their skills develop ask them to summarize the contents of a site or expect them to review and/or compare sites.

Here are some examples of research activities that a learner might undertake.

A *nursing* course

Compile an annotated list of web sites about basic chemistry that would be useful to the trainee nurse.

A *business* course

Locate two web sites on organizational behaviour and compare the usefulness of each to your particular business.

A *journalism* course

Choose a topical issue about a country other than your own, locate three online newspapers and produce a summary of their approach to this news story.

WRITTEN ASSIGNMENTS

Written assignments show what learners have learned from the course materials, from additional readings and from their own research. These assignments can be word-processed and e-mailed to you for feedback and comment. This feedback can be in an e-mail or directly on the word-processed document, perhaps distinguished from the student's work by a different font or colour. Some software allows comments to be added as a hyperlink or has some other feature that allows comments or annotations. Naturally both learner and tutor have to have the software with this feature.

Here are some examples of written assignments which actually differ little if at all from the sort of assignments you might set in a face-to-face course – it is the method of delivery to the tutor that is different.

An *environmental science* course

Word-process and e-mail to your tutor an essay which states how and why pollution, depletion and degradation of the physical environment occurs.

An *art theory* course

Produce as a web page an introduction to post-modernism with reference to three different media (such as film, television, painting, three-dimensional art). Your web page should include annotated links to other web sites about post-modernism. Post your web site as an attachment to the course conference.

A *law in the workplace* course

Read the Data Protection Act and produce an assignment that shows how your company is meeting the Act's requirements and make proposals about how your company could improve its data protection policies.

PRACTICAL WORK

This is one of the most challenging aspects of online learning, but don't dismiss the possibility. How can learners demonstrate practical activity online?

- By keeping a reflective diary which describes a process (baking a cake, creating an electrical circuit, serving a customer) then considering what has been learned.
- By taking photographs of the process (and sending them to you as attachments).
- By taking photographs of the product.
- By gathering eyewitness testaments from people who can observe the practical work locally.

For example:

An *institutional catering* course

Plan, cook and serve a three course meal suitable for a person with an allergy to dairy products. Keep a diary that describes and reflects on both the planning and the preparation stages of the process. Evaluate the process and the end product, incorporating feedback on the quality of the meal from the customer. E-mail this diary to your tutor.

A *bar workers'* course

Ask your bar manager to spend 10 minutes at the end of each shift giving you feedback on your work that day and record his/her comments on the proforma that you can download from the course web site. E-mail the completed proformas to your tutor.

A *materials science* course

Photograph local examples of the effect of pollution and weather on various types of stone. E-mail four examples of these photographs to your tutor and to your learning set with an accompanying explanation which states the stone type, how pollution/weather has impacted on the stone, and what steps could be taken to prevent further deterioration.

WHOLE GROUP DISCUSSION

Distance education need no longer be an isolated endeavour as group interactions can easily be incorporated into web courses. Discussion can be conducted via e-mail or using a conferencing system. Ensure your course builds in activities that allow your learners to share and develop their ideas with others in the course. This could include brainstorming, debating and discussion. Group processes will be discussed further in Chapter 11.

Examples of whole group activities:

A *media* course

'What value is there in studying advertisements?' Discuss in the course conference.

A *marketing* course

'What impact will increasing confidence in Internet security have on online shopping?' Initiate or contribute to a discussion in the course conference during Week 4. Include hyperlinks in your message to web sites that support any points that you make.

A *tourism* course

A topic sub-conference has been set up. Within the next 72 hours a brainstorm will be held. As a whole group you should come up with as many ideas as possible about advice you would give to tourists intending to travel to world trouble spots. After 72 hours the tutor will produce a report based on the brainstorm and post it to the conference.

SMALL GROUP WORK

Learners can also be given tasks to complete in groups and in pairs. They could work on projects that require investigation and then negotiation, which will lead to an agreed outcome.

Examples of small group activities:

A *foreign language* course

Post a 150-word autobiography to your learning set's sub-conference in the target language. Post at least three follow up messages commenting or seeking clarification upon the other autobiographies.

A *film studies* course

Within the next 48 hours download the Martin Scorsese quiz from the course web site and with your pair find out the answers and post them to the course conference.

A *creative writing* course

Your learning set should agree to research one of the following poetic forms: sonnet, haiku, limerick. Your set should produce a single document with a short introduction to the form and at least one example of original work that you have produced which illustrates this form. The person in your set whose name is nearest the start of the alphabet should coordinate this.

Tutorials

In a face-to-face course tutorials take a variety of forms. They might involve the tutor walking round a class talking one to one to learners who need help, they might be a few words exchanged at the end of a class or there may be a system of regular tutorial slots built into the timetable. In each case the purpose of tutorials is for both tutor and learner to raise concerns and seek resolutions and they can occur just as easily online as face to face. Learners may wish to ask for clarification about the course content, or to know if their work is meeting the course requirements. They may want to discuss something that is affecting their work – a personal or economic problem. Or they may need help organizing their workload or planning their time. You may wish to check understanding and give advice about additional activities a learner could undertake to reinforce what has been learned. It may be necessary to remind the learner of what is expected in terms of standards of work or meeting deadlines.

Assessment

In most courses it is expected that some sort of assessment will take place. Assessment has three possible functions. First, it enables the tutor, and the learner, to monitor progress and thus identify any strengths or weaknesses in the student's work. This is called diagnostic assessment. Second, it provides an opportunity for the tutor to give the learner feedback. This is called formative assessment. Third, it is a way of meeting the requirements of accrediting or awarding bodies in order that learners can receive a qualification. This is called summative assessment. In practice the different functions of assessment are not clear-cut but properly overlap and integrate.

Much of the diagnostic and formative assessment can be informal – given through feedback on students' work and in tutorials. Peer assessment may also be a useful tool for determining progress. It may be desirable to build more formal assessment points into the course as well. Any activity that has an outcome that can be measured objectively could be used for such an assessment. Software is available to help you construct such assessment activities as quizzes or multiple-choice tests which can give an immediate automated response.

The summative assessments may depend on the requirements of an external body. There may be a terminal examination, for example, or a requirement that the learner produces a portfolio of coursework to particular specifications. If you as tutor are at liberty to determine what constitutes the summative assessment then you will have already decided which are the key activities that will evidence achievement when you were establishing the assessment criteria.

When determining what work is to be assessed the questions to ask are:

- Will this assessment provide me with the information I need about a student's progress towards and achievement of the course's learning outcomes?
- Is the method of this assessment the best way of harvesting this information?
- Is this assessment a useful exercise from the student's point of

view – does it reinforce or extend skills, knowledge or understanding? Will it increase the student's confidence and independence?

- Is this assessment going to contribute to the student's final mark or qualification on the course?
- Is this assessment essential?

8 THE WEB AS A RESOURCE

Although you may choose to supplement your course materials in some way, perhaps with video or hardcopy books, most of your course materials will be mounted on the Web as web pages. This means that as well as the course materials you have written yourself you will be able to include hyperlinks, which will allow your learners to click on to the grandest accumulation of resources that has ever been available to the tutor. This chapter helps you make good use of those resources by pointing you in the direction of good web sites, and then explains how you go about distinguishing between the good sites and the poor when you search for your links. Understanding the factors that make for good course design will not only help you enrich your course materials by ensuring that the sites you link to are good, it will also inform your judgements about the design of your own web materials.

Resources on the web that support education and training

As a tutor you will want to find resources that will be useful to you and to your learners. You can include hyperlinks to sites that will enhance your course by providing background reading and examples, or use web sites as the basis for learner activities. As well as being a terrific source of information, many web sites offer opportunities for interaction and communication which can be developed into valuable and exciting learning experiences for your learners. There are lots of free things for you and your learners to download and use too.

As well as exploring the Web for possible link material, this section will also point you towards sites that will make you better informed. This section cannot hope to direct you to all the useful sites on the Web that are available to support your teaching, nor can it hope to cover all the subject areas that potential online tutors might wish to teach. But what it does aim to do is give you a flavour of what is out there so that when you are doing your own searching you have some idea of what you might be able to find that is appropriate to your educational or training needs. Note: web sites come and go, I am afraid. I have selected sites that seem to be well established, but if you should find that the web address no longer works, try using a search engine to search on the web site's title.

A special plea

The generosity and open-handedness of the Internet community amazes and delights me. As well as thinking about the ways that you can use the resources that are available to you, try too to think about how you can make your contribution to the Internet community.

INFORMATION AND COMMUNICATIONS TECHNOLOGY

Unsurprisingly, the Internet is an excellent source of information about itself. There is also plenty of free software available on the web.

Cern
http://www.cern.ch/

The web site of the organization that laid the foundations for the web as we know it today.

Living IT
http://www.living-it.org.uk/

Short online courses teaching various Internet skills, including learning on the Internet.

Webwise
http://www.bbc.co.uk/education/webwise/

The BBC's guide to the web. Introductory information, plus a panel of experts to whom you can e-mail queries.

Parents Information Network
http://www.pin-parents.com/index.htm

Aims to enable parents to become informed purchasers and more confident, effective users of new technology by providing unbiased information and advice. Very useful for non-parents too.

Completely Free Software
http://www.completelyfreesoftware.com/

A wide selection of software downloads, including word processors, photo-editing, typing tutors and games. Good choice of Internet related software.

ENGLISH DICTIONARIES AND THESAURI

There are plenty of these – many are standard dictionaries that simply give definitions. Others have additional features such as the inclusion of sound if you need to know how a word should be pronounced, word games and word of the day (as I write it is 'hoary' meaning 'gray or white with or as if with age'). There is a range of some more specialist in nature such as rhyming dictionaries, dictionaries of unusual and preposterous words, dictionaries of alliteration and acronym and synonym dictionaries. Look under the Reference category of Yahoo or do a search using the keyword **Dictionaries**.

Dictionary Com
http://www.dictionary.com/

Simple and uncomplicated – recommended for people who want just plain definitions and an example of the word in context.

Merrion-Webster Dictionary
http://www.m-w.com/dictionary.htm

Offering a more sophisticated service, including a brief history of the English language, a guide to international business communications and a thesaurus.

Project Bartleby
http://www.columbia.edu/acis/bartleby/

A collection of pre-twentieth century quotations, searchable by word.

Roget's Thesaurus
http://www.thesaurus.com

As it says on its home page 'Words are our precision tools. Imprecision engenders ambiguity and hours are wasted in removing verbal misunderstandings.' An excellent point to bear in mind when writing online course materials.

FOREIGN LANGUAGE DICTIONARIES AND TRANSLATORS

There are a huge number of foreign language dictionaries available, for all the major languages and many minority ones, including several of which I, to be honest, have never heard. Some will just translate single words, others are capable of translating several paragraphs. A service provided by Alta Vista also allows you to enter a web address and it will translate the whole web page into (or from) several European languages including English, French, German and Portuguese. These translators should be treated with a degree of caution as the translations are generated electronically and do not handle idioms well. Many search engines also have country-specific versions which may be useful as sources of information about particular countries.

Internet Press
http://gallery.uunet.be/internetpress/diction.htm

This is an excellent starting point because it provides links to a vast collection of foreign language dictionaries (including a German–Welsh and a Kanienkehaka–English).

Logos Dictionary
http://www.logos.it/index.html

A constantly growing dictionary of translations, now getting on for 8 million entries (all languages). An example of a project you could contribute to if you were a linguist.

Alta Vista

http://www.altavista.com/

This is Alta Vista's main page – look for the AV translation services link. Try translating a phrase into a foreign language, then back into English. English to Italian and back again turned 'The old man kicked the bucket on Thursday' to 'The old man has given of soccer to the bucket Thursday.' I see.

Yahoo

http://www.yahoo.co.uk/

Yahoo's main page with links to 15 or more of its world Yahoos.

ART GALLERIES AND MUSEUMS

Most of the major art galleries are now online, as well as many fascinating but rather obscure and unusual ones such as the Museum of Bad Art. The internationally known museums all have a virtual presence, as do specialist ones such as the Museum of the Romanian Peasant. Many museums offer additional services that are particularly useful to tutors.

The Louvre

http://mistral.culture.fr/louvre/louvrea.htm

Includes a virtual tour (though you will need to download a Quicktime viewer for that).

Comlab

http://www.comlab.ox.ac.uk/archive/other/museums/galleries.html

An eclectic collection of links to art galleries and the services they offer.

The Metropolitan Museum of Modern Art, New York

http://www.metmuseum.org/

Good educational services, such as an exploration of portrait painting which allows you to click on a portrait and get an analysis of the painter's intentions.

The Science Museum
http://www.nmsi.ac.uk/

Information about the museum's exhibitions and collection, and the STEM Project which encourages the development and sharing, through the Web, of educational resources that have been written by teachers and students.

The British Museum
http://www.british-museum.ac.uk/index.html

The museum that houses 6.5 million objects ranging in size from sherds to colossal statues.

NEWS SERVICES

As well as providing up-to-the-minute news services you will find excellent databases of back articles and features. Many of the world's newspapers are now available. As well as the usual headlines and news coverage you may find the same sort of features as in a print copy of the paper, such as jobs, property sales, fashion, weather, horoscopes and obituaries.

BBC News
http://news.bbc.co.uk/

News service frequently updated throughout the day. It includes video and sound using Real Audio. Links to other BBC news services such as sport and business.

The Guardian
http://www.guardian.co.uk/

You will need to register, but it is free and gives access to news and articles. It has a section called The Talk where you can post messages to other *Guardian* readers.

The Washington Post
http://washingtonpost.com/

The newspaper of the capital city of the most powerful country on earth so it is probably worth finding out what its world view is.

The St Petersburg Times
http://www.sptimes.ru/

The English-language newspaper of St Petersburg, Russia which has been online since 1994. Very impressive.

ONLINE MAGAZINES AND JOURNALS

The Node
http://node.on.ca/

A site devoted to articles and discussion to promote informed decisions about learning technologies.

Arts and Letters Daily
http://www.cybereditions.com/aldaily/

This site provides links to a huge variety of articles harvested from international online news and articles. It is updated daily (well, six times a week).

Nationalgeographic.com
http://www.nationalgeographic.com/index.html

The online presence of the National Geographic Society.

Educom Review
http://www.educause.edu/pub/er/erm.html

Exploring the changing ways we will work, learn and communicate in the digital world of the twenty-first century.

The Economist
http://www.economist.com/

An international weekly journal of news, ideas, opinions and articles. Includes an archive of articles dating back to 1995.

BIOGRAPHIES

Who's virtually who? Real life and fictional, world famous and completely unheard of – they're all on the Internet.

My Hero
http://www.myhero.com/

Look up the biography of a hero, or add your own hero (it could be your mum).

Biography.com
http://www.biography.com/

Celebrating celebrities as diverse as Virginia Woolf and Evel Knievel. Search their database of 20 000 biographies.

LESSON PLANS

What more can a tutor ask for? There are several sites that offer a collection of lesson plans for all subjects and for all levels. Many of these are intended for face-to-face delivery, but for lessons aimed at older learners there are plenty that can be put to use for online purposes. There are also opportunities for tutors to add their own lesson plans. All the sites I located are American – what does this tell us about British teachers?

The Gateway
http://thegateway.org/simple1.html

You can browse by subject or by keyword to locate lesson plans and various other educational resources for all subjects and age groups.

The Lesson Plans Page
http://www.lessonplanspage.com/

This claims to be the largest collection of lesson plans (300) on the Internet, though it is aimed mainly at younger children.

Ask Eric Lesson Plans
http://ericir.syr.edu/Virtual/Lessons/

This perhaps is the largest collection with more than a thousand lesson plans available.

Microsoft Class Resources
http://www.microsoft.com/education/curric/activity/

Glossy and well produced, but assumes access to various Microsoft products such as Encarta and World Atlas.

FREE PICTURES AND CLIP ART

There are sites that offer copyright free pictures which can enhance your teaching materials (useful for adding to hardcopy handouts as well as putting on web pages). If you don't have the time, talent or software to produce icons, buttons, animations, backgrounds and horizontal bars for your own web pages then there are sites that let you download them for free, usually only asking that their use be acknowledged. There are also plenty of free tutorials giving advice about how to create and edit graphics.

Barry's Clip Art Server
http://www.barrysclipart.com/

A collection of clip art plus links to other collections, and free e-postcards plus helpful advice about incorporating clip art into your web pages.

Clip Art Castle
http://www.clipartcastle.com/

Thousands of free graphics on various themes, including Gothic, Egyptian and space.

DISCUSSION LISTS AND NEWSGROUPS

If you want to talk to other tutors about your specialist subject, or you want your learners to participate in discussion outside your course group then there is a good chance that there is an e-mail list or newsgroup that you can join. If not, start one.

Liszt
http://www.liszt.com/

This is the best starting point for locating potential discussions. It has a directory of 90 095 e-mail discussion lists and 30 000 Usenet Newsgroups.

Netiquette Home Page
http://www.fau.edu/netiquette/net/netiquette.html

Once you have located a likely list or newsgroup, this site will tell you how to behave properly in your communications.

ARTS AND HUMANITIES

Literature is very well represented on the web with many full classic texts available. Some sites offer the opportunity for learners to discuss characters, plots and themes. Students of cinema will find plenty of sites for both information and interactivity, such as opportunities to include their own film reviews. For the art teacher there are the art galleries and museums discussed above. I won't pretend that a virtual art gallery or museum is as good as visiting the real thing, but it does enable you and your learners to view works and objects that would otherwise only be available via field trips or in expensive art books. Some enthusiastic amateurs have produced some excellent sites that are well worth a look. There are some comprehensive history sites and the Internet is proving a huge boon to family historians.

British Literature
http://www.britishliterature.com/

British Literature aims to be a comprehensive (and entertaining) resource for British Literature fans, students and teachers, and for Anglophiles in general.

World Wide Arts Resources
http://wwar.com/

Offers a 'definitive, interactive gateway to all exemplars of qualitative arts information and culture on the Internet'.

Kodak Limited
http://www.kodak.co.uk/

As well as providing commercial services, Kodak offers 'tips, techniques and tutorials'. The Quilt Project is shaping up to an interesting collection of personal photographs and stories.

The National Museum of Photography, Film and Television
http://www.nmsi.ac.uk/nmpft/

Has a wonderful collection of links to sites round the world.

Britannia Historical Documents
http://britannia.com/history/docs/

A collection of documents relevant to the history of England and Wales, from the confession of St Patrick (fifth century) to the Yalta Conference Agreement (1945).

Family Search
http://www.familysearch.org/

Allows you to search for your ancestors in the database of the Church of Jesus Christ of Latter-day Saints.

SOCIETY

Whatever 'ology' you specialize in, or whatever cultural or interest group you belong to, it is almost certain to be represented.

Social Science Information gateway (SOSIG)
http://sosig.esrc.bris.ac.uk/

SOSIG offers social scientists a quick and easy way of finding quality networked information to support their work.

Web Content Accessibility Guidelines
http://www.w3.org/TR/WAI-WEBCONTENT/

A comprehensive site hosted by the World Wide Web Consortium which addresses the issue of making web design fully accessible to people with disabilities. Don't start any web authoring till you have read it.

The British Council
http://www.britcoun.org/

Describes the work of the British Council in promoting Britain both in the UK and around the world.

The Ringing World
http://www.luna.co.uk/~ringingw/

The weekly journal for churchbell ringers.

SCIENCE, TECHNOLOGY AND MATHEMATICS

From the earth's inner core to the furthest reach of the universe, it is all online. Also help with hard sums.

The Guardian Online
http://www.newsunlimited.co.uk/The_Paper/Online/

For coverage of IT, science and technology. Intelligent and unhysterical coverage of Internet issues.

TechNet
http://www.worldbank.org/html/fpd/technet/

An initiative of the World Bank to encourage and promote the use of science, technology and information in development.

How Stuff Works
http://www.howstuffworks.com/

A thoroughly entertaining site which answers all those questions you have always wanted to ask such as 'What's chewing gum made of?', 'How does a cruise missile work?' and 'What's inside a bathroom scale?'

NASA
http://www.hq.nasa.gov/

Home page of the National Aeronautics and Space Administration. The link to their education programme is particularly interesting.

PASS Maths
http://pass.maths.org.uk/index.html

Newsletter for the mathematically minded from the University of Cambridge.

TRAVEL

There is plenty for the traveller. Translation services are discussed above. Travel agents have made their presence felt and travel arrangements, including the buying of foreign currency, can be arranged online. Most countries now use the Web to publicize tourist information and there are many 'unofficial' tourist sites with entertaining and off-beat information. You can also find plenty of maps, weather forecasts and time zone converters.

Thomas Cook
http://www.thomascook.co.uk/

Book your tickets and order your currency with one of the worlds oldest travel companies, all online.

Visit Britain
http://www.visitbritain.com/

The official site of the British Tourist Authority. Reasonably comprehensive information for the visitor to Britain, including facts and figures sections.

Rough Guides
http://travel.roughguides.com/

An online version of the useful guide for the independent traveller. Covers more than 4 000 locations.

The Universal Currency Converter
http://www.xe.net/currency/

Convert almost any world currency to almost any other world currency. Rates updated every 15 minutes.

BUSINESS AND MANAGEMENT

One of the advantages of the Internet is that international financial information can be so frequently updated.

Bank of England
http://www.bankofengland.co.uk/

The Old Lady of Threadneedle Street's site. Monetary and statistical links and such delights as the latest minutes of the Monetary Policy Committee.

Business Information Sources on the Internet
http://www.dis.strath.ac.uk/business/index.html

The University of Strathclyde's selective guide to Internet sites that contain business information, with emphasis on UK sources.

The Biz
http://www.thebiz.co.uk/

The Business Information Zone is for users seeking UK-relevant business information, products and services on the Internet.

Yahoo Finance
http://finance.uk.yahoo.com/

Up-to-the-minute information on stocks and shares, foreign exchange rates, business news, company profiles.

Biz/ed
http://bized.ac.uk/

A unique business and economics service for students, teachers and lecturers. Superb learning materials, such as the virtual 11 Downing Street where you can have a go at keeping the economy on track.

Business Link
http://www.businesslink.co.uk/

Advice for businesses great and small on business plans, marketing, staff development, innovation and much, much more.

Edward de Bono's Authorized Web Site
http://www.edwdebono.co.uk/debono/home.htm

The guru of creative thinking in management who claims he is 'one of the very few people in history to have had a major impact on the way we think – rather than on what we think.'

FT Mastering Management
http://www.ftmastering.com/

Management theory, practice and case studies from the *Financial*

Times. Lots of useful information free, though you have to pay a subscription fee to access the whole site.

GOVERNMENT

The UK government has followed the lead of the USA, and now has most if not all of its government departments online.

10 Downing Street
http://www.number-10.gov.uk/index.html

A source of government news, information and a virtual tour of the house, though I couldn't find the toilet.

The White House
http://www.whitehouse.gov/WH/Welcome.html

E-mail the President of the USA, his wife, or look at pictures of his pets (four-legged).

Department of Education and Employment
http://www.dfee.gov.uk/

Vast collection of resources with links to the University of Industry, Lifelong Learning and National Grid for Learning sites.

Inland Revenue
http://www.inlandrevenue.gov.uk/home.htm

Featuring news and information on tax and national insurance matters in the United Kingdom.

Houses of Parliament
http://www.parliament.uk/

Find information about the United Kingdom Parliament, the House of Commons and the House of Lords, including an online Hansard.

LAW

Stay on the right side of the law by keeping yourself informed.

The Law Society
http://www.lawsoc.org.uk/

The professional body for English and Welsh solicitors, acting as a regulator, campaigner and service provider.

UK Legal
http://www.uklegal.com/

Links to UK and worldwide legal resources.

Journal of Information, Law & Technology
http://elj.warwick.ac.uk/jilt/default.htm

An online journal with articles that examine the legal implications of living in a networked society.

The Office of Data Protection
http://www.open.gov.uk/dpr/dprhome.htm

News, guidance and a summary, as well as the Act itself.

I hope you enjoy seeking out useful sites for your online teaching and learning.

Evaluating web sites

You will have had fun visiting some of the sites that I have directed you to in this chapter, and finding sites of your own with your searches. You will have discovered that the Web is a wonderfully democratic publishing medium where multinational companies which command budgets of billions have to take their place besides individuals with some spare time, some free software and stacks of enthusiasm. It takes little technical skill to produce a web page with a professional gloss, and there is not necessarily any editorial control over the content and style of a web site. Moreover, space on the Web to mount pages is obtainable cheaply or free. This has led to the diversity that is so much part of the Web's appeal. It does, of course, have its downside. You must be very careful to discriminate between what is valuable and what is complete rubbish. And don't imagine that it is the multinationals that are producing the quality web sites and the keen amateurs that are producing the rubbish – you may find that is just as likely to be the reverse.

This section provides you with some guidelines to enable you to conduct your searches with a critical eye. You should look at the web sites carefully and evaluate their quality, particularly if you are looking for sites to link to from your own web pages as you don't want to waste your learners' time on poorly written and constructed sites. Take the following factors into account when you make your judgement.

Purpose	Who is the site aimed at? What is the site's purpose? Does the site's author, or its sponsors, have any vested interests that might lead to bias?
Content	Is the information accurate? What is the quality of the proofreading: are there typos, spelling errors or poor grammar? Is the style, tone and language used appropriate for the target audience and for the site's purpose? Does it use jargon inappropriately? Is it interesting, entertaining, engaging? How does the site compare to others on the same subject?
Authority	Who wrote the content of the web page? Do they have the necessary expertise? Are you told their credentials, or is there a pointer to where this information can be found? Is contact information available? Is the author working independently or does he/she represent a company, an academic body, a government, a charity or an interest group?

Currency	Is the site dated?
	Has the site been updated recently and, if not, does that matter?
	If it is a new site, is it likely to be available for the duration of your course?
Appearance	Is the site pleasing to look at?
	Is there clutter, crowding and clashing colours?
	Do the graphics enhance the site by illustrating the content?
	Does it include features that might be distracting, such as animations, flashing text, advertising?
	Are icons easy to interpret?
Navigability	Is it easy to find your way to the parts of the site you want to locate?
	Can you find your way back to the home/index page?
	Do all the internal links (links within the web site) work?
	Are all the links to other sites reliable?
	Are the links to other sites useful?
	Are these links annotated or organized into categories in any way?
	If frames are used, do they make the site easier to navigate?
Other	Would a person with a specific disability be able to use the site?
	Is the print large? Is there a text alternative to graphics?
	Do sound, video and other technical features add to the usefulness of the site?
	Does the site require additional software/hardware to use?
	Are there elements that slow down the loading of the site to an unacceptable level?
	Are any interactive features straightforward to use?

Copyright

The Internet community is one of the most generous I have come across and its willingness to share expertise must be cherished. Since the world's lawyers have yet to agree on appropriate copyright laws for the Internet I cannot give you any guidance that I can guarantee will keep you out of the courts. However, I will suggest that before you use any materials you find on the Web, or before you link to any web pages, give some thought to the possibility that you might be breaking the law, or at least abusing someone's good will. If you wish to use information you have gleaned from a web site then cite your source. If you wish to set up a link to another web site, then ask permission if you can. If it is refused then don't link, if conditions are imposed (such as linking to the main page rather than some other page on the site) then adhere to them.

Citing Internet sources

You would (I hope) naturally cite hardcopy sources if you were reproducing somebody else's concepts and ideas, statistics and facts in any of your own course materials. The same applies when using sources from the Internet. As yet, no single standard has emerged as being universally accepted. However, here are the main elements that should be included:

- Author – This information is not always included on every page of a web site so look on other pages to find it. If you cannot locate the author then include the name of the organization responsible for the site. You may also need to include information here about the origin of the source.
- Title – This should appear on the web page, or if it doesn't look at the browser's title bar.
- Date – A well-designed web page will include the date on which it was last updated. If it doesn't, and there is no other indication of its date, then use the date that you last saw it on the Web.
- URL – Include the whole of the URL, including the http:// bit. Use angle brackets (<>) to separate the URL from other punctuation so as not to cause confusion.

Here are some examples:

K. Offley and A. Massey *An Examination of the Feeding Behaviour of Sea Mammals* (August 1999) <http://www.mass.ac.uk/biol/seamammal/food.html>

Morris Faulkner *Talking with Fathers and Sons* (Accessed 19 August 1999) <http://www.samson.com/parents/fathers.html>

9
DESIGNING YOUR COURSE FOR THE INTERNET

It is outside the remit of this book to teach the technicalities of web authoring. However, as an online tutor you may well be involved in decisions about the development of web-based materials and there are issues of which you need to be aware. It is useful for you to have some understanding of the language used in writing web pages and be mindful of what to take into account when deciding on such things as the layout, appearance and navigation of your web pages and site. This section starts with a general introduction to hypertext markup language.

Hypertext markup language

Hypertext markup language, known as HTML, is the language in which all web pages are written. It is not a programming language and needs no special software to produce. Rather it is a series of coded tags which are inserted into a plain text document so that when that text document is loaded into a browser it will be interpreted as a web page. Thus what appears in a plain text editor (Figure 9.1) will look very different in a browser (Figure 9.2).

There is a large and ever-growing number of tags that can tell the browser such things as how big to display the heading; the background colour of the page; when to start a new paragraph; and when to create a link to other files such as graphics, documents or sound. If you want to see what HTML looks like, load any web page into your browser then look at the Source Code. Exactly how you do this will depend upon which browser you use, but you will certainly be able to find it if you explore the menus on your browser's menu bar. You will see the text of the web page plus lots of tags which look something like this: </H1>. The strength of

Figure 9.1 Hypertext markup language

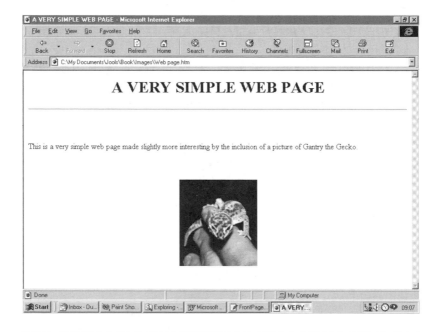

Figure 9.2 A simple web page

HTML is that it is platform independent – this means it can be interpreted by any browser on any computer. Web pages using HTML can be created with the simplest text editor (such as Notepad). However, if you wish to create anything more than the most basic of web pages then you will need to invest a great deal of time in learning the principles and practice of HTML. It may well be that your time is better spent on the pedagogy of your course design rather than the technicalities, and that HTML is left to a specialist.

A variety of WYSIWYG (what you see is what you get) web authoring programs are now available. You can buy dedicated web authoring programmes such as Microsoft's Frontpage or SoftQuad's Hotmetal Pro, or obtain more basic programs for free. Increasingly ordinary desktop publishing or word-processing programs will also allow you to create web pages without having to learn HTML. I should say though that experienced web authors would question the value of some of these products, claiming that the quality of the HTML may be compromised. This has implications for your learners. Web pages that do not adhere to accepted standards may not render properly, or at all, in the browser that they are using.

Designing a good web site

Whether you are authoring your own pages or employing someone to do it for you, it is important that what is finally produced is of the highest standard in terms of content, navigational ease and appearance.

Before you or your web author start writing any HTML, plan, on paper, what you want to do. Consider what information you need to produce for your learners. Be creative. Your course will be a dreary experience if all you do is reproduce a set of lecture notes. Include opportunities for your learners to look at other web sites, talk to other learners and participate actively.

CONVERTED/ORIGINAL MATERIALS

If you are converting an existing course look through your course materials to select what needs to be turned into web form. If starting from scratch then make notes about what original content you need to develop yourself. Any materials you produce in plain text on a word processor can easily be converted into HTML at a later stage.

ADDITIONAL RESOURCES

Start to compile an annotated list of useful links to other web resources that you may wish to include. Do not include any links that are not of a high standard.

If it is necessary to incorporate any other resources such as graphics, sound or downloadable text files get them converted into a format that a browser can recognize.

LEARNER ACTIVITY

Plan how and at what points you need to include learner activities such as tasks or assignments.

STRUCTURE

Think about how the course is to be structured. Determine how you expect your learners to progress through the course. Is it to be linear with all learners completing sections in the same order, or do you want your learners to select their own path through the course?

ADDITIONAL INFORMATION

Think about what other information is needed such as the course outline, course timetable, tutor contact details, technical information, expectation and responsibilities of learners. Include a copyright statement.

CONTENT

Two very important factors need to be taken into account: 1) your learners will be at a distance from you; and 2) your learners will be reading from a computer screen.

Language and tone

● Your web pages should be written in clear and unambiguous

language which is at an appropriate level for your target learners. Remember that unambiguity is crucial – you will not have the opportunity, as in class, to correct misunderstandings as soon as they arise.

- If you are targeting an international audience avoid idioms or jokes that may be incomprehensible to people whose first language is different to yours, or who have different cultural expectations.
- If you use any technical language then explain its meaning when you introduce it, or provide a glossary (you can use hyperlinks to the glossary) so that clicking on a technical term will immediately take your learner to its definition.

Structuring content

- Reading from the screen is a different experience to reading from hard copy. It helps the reader if the text content is broken up into sections with headings and sub-headings. Bulleted and numbered lists work well on web sites.
- The topic of each web page should be clear as soon as a page is loaded, so ensure that any page heading is self-explanatory or that an introductory paragraph is at the top of the page.

HYPERLINKS

Place links carefully. State clearly what learners will find when they click on that link so that they can decide whether they need to go there directly or read the rest of your page before exploring the links. Distinguish between links that you regard as essential to your learners' understanding and those that are optional.

PROOFREAD

Proofread your web pages to ensure that they are all accurate. The standard of spelling and grammar on the Web is not high but, as a tutor, please do not think that such low standards are acceptable to you. Remember that sloppy web pages will undermine your learners' faith in the quality of the tuition that you are offering. Get someone else to proofread your pages too – they will spot inconsistencies, errors and ambiguities that you may miss.

NAVIGATION, NAVIGATION, NAVIGATION

What use will your web site be if your learners are unable to find their way round it? Navigation around your web site must be foolproof.

INDEX PAGE

Include an index page that can act as a starting point for your learners and can be returned to from every page on your site. This index page should give an overview of the whole course by including a list of contents, plus links to any other important sections such as the course conference, a FAQ (Frequently Asked Questions) page or a course timetable.

BUTTONS AND BARS

Keep such navigational buttons and bars neat and small. Use them in a consistent way across your site. Provide links as text as well as buttons and bars.

PAGE LENGTH

There are different schools of thought about the 'right' length of a web page. Some people think that users do not like to scroll, so very long web pages should be split into smaller linked web pages. Others think that too much clicking back and forth confuses the users and so are happy to have long pages and let users scroll. You must decide for yourself what will best suit you and your learners. However, if a web page is long include internal page links so that learners can quickly hop to any point in the page they need. Also include links (say, after each section) that will take your learners back to the top of the page. A long web page is anything longer than three screens. If you decide to break up content into smaller 'chunks' then it may also be a good idea to provide a version that can be printed out as one long page.

FRAMES

Frames are a feature of many web sites. They subdivide the browser window into two or more sub-windows, each displaying a different web page. It may be possible to scroll up or down each frame individually or to resize each frame (or they may be fixed).

They are often used to display a list of contents down one side of the screen which allows the contents to stay in view. Clicking on an item on the contents list will load the chosen page into the other sub-window. Although there are some advantages to using frames both to enhance appearance and to aid navigation, treat them with enormous caution for they bring in their wake many problems. They load slowly, they do not look good on small monitors, and cause problems when printed, saved or added to bookmarks/favourites. It is not even always apparent if frames are being used or not, so users may think that they have saved some useful piece of information to their own computer when all they have saved is an advert which has been put into its own frame! Frames do not work on all browsers. Think very seriously about whether they will add value to your site before you use them.

COMPATIBILITY AND USABILITY

You may not know what equipment your learners will use to view your web site. Bear in mind that there are various versions of different browsers and so your web pages need to be properly rendered whatever browser is used. Note also that monitor size varies. Your learner may be gazing at a 19 inch screen or squinting at a palm-sized screen. So try out your web pages on a variety of browsers and with different size monitors before you launch your course.

Check your web pages with an HTML validator (there are several web sites offering this service free on the Web) to make sure that they comply with international HTML standards. This should mean that your web site will render properly whatever browser is used.

APPEARANCE

Naturally you will want your web site to look attractive, but content and navigational ease are a higher priority. Please do not make the mistake of thinking that the more pictures, icons, bars, colours and animated gifs you use the lovelier it will be. It will not. It will be messy, confusing and slow to load. It is less likely to be compatible with all browsers. Use these enhancements, but use them sparingly – they should only be used to illustrate and illuminate the content or to aid navigation. You may find web designers are keen to show off their skills by incorporating a plethora of such fancy features. Do not allow yourself to be persuaded.

UNIFORMITY

Ensure that there is some sort of house style across your web site, using a common colour scheme, logo, background or layout. This will help your learners distinguish between the course materials that you have provided and links to other sites.

COLOUR AND SPACE

Use colour and space wisely. Have a look at other web sites to see what colour schemes seem pleasing to you. Your learners may be looking at your pages for some time so avoid anything too lurid such as bright pink on black. Use enough space around the text to aid readability but remember that too much space means learners will feel cheated when they start printing things off and find only a quarter of the printed pages have anything on them; too little space and your pages will be difficult to read. Don't use a background graphic that is distracting or makes the text hard to read.

GRAPHICS

Only use graphics if they are essential as they will slow down the loading of your pages. Keep any you use small and relevant. Provide text alternatives as this means that if your learners have the graphics turned off they will get instead a short label which tells them what the graphic is. They can then load the picture if they need to see it. It may also be that one of your learners is sight impaired and relies on a browser that reads aloud the content including these text alternatives.

ANIMATIONS

What may seem charming and amusing when first seen can quickly lose its appeal. Though animations may work well on sites where the user is not expected to stick around, they can become irritating when looked at for any length of time. Animations can have real educational value, for example to demonstrate a simple process, and they may enhance a page where you wouldn't expect a learner to stay for long, but don't use them otherwise.

ADVANCED TECHNICAL FEATURES

Java applets, Active X, image maps and other advanced design features are best left to the experts. Remember, the fancier your web site, the more likelihood there is that your learners will have problems of access. Keep it simple.

Maintaining your web site

Once your web site is ready it can be uploaded on to the server. But your job does not finish there – you need to go back to the web site to make sure that it continues to work well.

CHECK LINKS

Develop a routine for checking that all the internal and external links are working on your web site and repair or replace any broken links you identify as soon as possible. If you know that it may take a few days to replace a link with one equally useful then let your learners know immediately that you are aware of the broken link and give them a time scale for replacing it.

MAKING CHANGES

One of the advantages of publishing your course on the Web is that it can be easily adapted and revised. Once the course has started it may be necessary to make changes and improvements. Remember though that your learners may have already saved the course to their own computer or printed pages off. If important changes have been made to your course then alert learners to the need to update the pages they already have.

DATE

Somewhere on each web page include the date when it was last updated, and make sure you change it when any alterations are made. This is so your learners can check they are looking at the latest version of each page.

Educational courseware

There is now available a range of commercial courseware that provides toolboxes for the creation of a total educational environment and assists those with few technical skills to design, deliver and administer online courses. WebCT, Merlin World Class, TopClass and Lotus LearningSpace are some examples. Such courseware provides features and tools which will facilitate:

- the generation of web pages and a navigational structure;
- communications such as e-mail messaging and conferencing systems, synchronous chat, group project organization;
- learning such as auto-marked multiple-choice tests, interactive case studies, learner tracking systems, library database creation;
- administration such as a course calendar, student records.

These companies have their own web sites where you can find out exactly what range of features are offered. It may also be possible to download trial versions, or to see examples in action.

PART *IV*

Getting your course up and running

10 PREPARING DELIVERY

Now you have everything in place, you have planned a wonderful course and you have built (or had built) the web site you need to start delivering it. Are you ready to go? Well, not quite; you need to ensure that you have the right environment to deliver your course, and the right cohort of learners to deliver it to.

Support from your organization

It is important that the organization within which you work recognizes that the demands of being an online tutor are somewhat different to those of a face-to-face tutor. You will need particular kinds of practical support and resources in order to make your course a success. Your key needs are:

- a fair allocation of time
- a comfortable and peaceful working environment
- adequate technology
- speedy technical support.

TIME

I fear that many organizations will see online tuition as a way of increasing tutor : learner ratios. Be clear, it is not. Tutors will need at least as much time for preparation, class contact and marking as in traditional teaching. In fact you and your employers need to remember that issues that can be resolved in seconds in a face-to-face classroom will almost inevitably take longer in the virtual classroom. There are several reasons for this, for example typing invariably takes longer than talking, clarifications may take several e-mails.

It is also highly likely that you will find yourself giving some technical support to your learners as well as course tuition.

Traditionally tutor time has been allocated in weekly blocks of an hour or two but you will find it works better online if you spread the tuition time over two or three sessions per week so that you do not have to face an overwhelming number of e-mails at one session and you can give speedy feedback to your learners.

WORK ENVIRONMENT

Online teaching needs to be conducted in a place where the tutor can concentrate without distractions. A busy learning centre, office, staffroom or library where there is background activity, ringing telephones and the potential for frequent interruption should be avoided. Many online tutors and their employers are happy to agree that online tuition should take place in the tutor's home. If this suits you then fine. There are many advantages for the tutor – a peaceful environment, no travel time and costs, familiar equipment, better coffee perhaps – but remember that you will also bear any additional costs of heating and lighting at home, not to mention an increased Internet access bill. There will also be some wear and tear on your home computer and you will need to buy more paper and printer ink. Make sure you come to a fair agreement in advance about any additional expenditure if you work from home.

A further consideration about home working is the need to make clear divisions about when you are at work and when you are not. Ideally the computer you work from should be in a room separate from your normal domestic activity so that you can close the door on it outside of work time (and keep your family or other residents out when you do want to work). If such separation is not possible then make clear decisions about what times you will allocate to your online work and stick to them. Three or four short sessions per week are preferable to one long one so that any learner e-mails receive a quick response.

TECHNOLOGY

Make sure that you have the technology to support your online work. You will need as a minimum:

- a fast computer;
- fast and reliable access to the Internet;
- an up-to-date browser;

- an e-mail system that allows you to create folders and sub-folders and to store e-mails;
- a good word processor;
- an up-to-date virus checker;
- any additional software that you will be using in your course.

And as well as making sure that you have the right hardware and software, make sure that you know how to use it.

If you are likely to be conducting the course in several places, ensure that the equipment you need is on all the computers you are using, and that you know how to transfer files and e-mails from one computer to another.

TECHNICAL SUPPORT

You must be prepared for the possibility that the technology may fail. Ensure that important files on your computer are backed up (such as any assignments you have received from your learners) or printed in hard copy (such as the contact details for your learners). If you are planning to conduct the course from one computer only, then have as back-up access to an alternative computer in case the one you usually use breaks down. If you don't have technical expertise yourself, make sure that you have quick access to a person who has. This will be necessary both for yourself and for technical problems that your learners will inevitably raise.

Marketing and recruiting

You may already have a group of learners in place, but if not you will need to recruit them. Obviously you will have done some market research before you started planning your course. Think again about the other courses that are similar to yours and focus your marketing on any unique features or particular strengths of your course such as any special expertise you may have in the field, or your organization's track record.

Consider the profiles of your potential learners – are most of them individuals, members of organizations or employees, or a mix of these? What influence does this have on how and where you wish to market your course? For example, individuals may be more interested in personal development or a skill that will help them change their career, an organization may be more interested in how a course will lead to a more skilled and productive workforce.

If you intend to run all or part of the course as a pilot initially you may want to recruit learners who are aware that the course is being tested and are willing to participate in the development of the course by providing constructive feedback. Such a group may be more tolerant of technical and other problems.

If the course is new then it may be worth keeping the price low for the first cohort or two. Learner satisfaction will be disseminated and as the reputation of your course grows you can increase the fees if you wish. Offer individuals incentives for introducing other learners to the course. Offer organizations discounts if they enrol several learners.

With online tuition you are not restricted to attracting learners from your own locality, so advertise nationally and internationally if the course you are teaching is appropriate.

The Web	Since your potential learners will need Internet access, the Web is a good place to advertise. Make sure you register your site with the main search engines so that potential learners looking for online courses will easily locate yours. There are also databases of online courses with which you can register. Your web site should give full information about the course, perhaps including sample sections. You should also include a contact e-mail address or an online form so the potential learner can request more information.
E-mail and newsgroups	You could also publicize your course with appropriate discussion lists and newsgroups, though you should first check that such advertising is acceptable.
Print media	You can, of course, advertise online courses alongside traditional courses in your prospectus, newsletters and leaflets. But also consider advertisements in national or international magazines that you think your potential learners may read. Perhaps relevant newspapers or magazines may be interested in running an article about your new course.
Personal contacts	Contact in person, by letter, e-mail, fax and phone, potential learners, either individuals or organizations that may be interested in providing cohorts on such courses.

Pre-course guidance

In a face-to-face course you are often able to meet and discuss the course with potential learners, and pointing them to the right course can usually be done successfully by matching their skills and aspirations to the courses you offer. However, learners are more likely to have selected themselves for traditional distance education courses. Online courses can build in some of the pre-course guidance that was formerly so difficult to incorporate in such distance courses.

Start by making it absolutely clear to learners what learning online will entail so that they will be able to judge if the course and its mode of delivery will meet their learning needs. Create a web page that is a first contact point for potential learners which will tell your learners what they need to know and will also promote your course. Include information on the following areas.

THE COURSE

- What the learner can expect to get out of the course such as skills, knowledge, personal or professional development, qualifications.
- The advantages of learning online.
- The course aims and learning outcomes.
- A description of the content of the course, perhaps including sample web pages to give a flavour of the content.
- Who will be tutoring the course, including a brief summary of their skills and qualifications.
- Any qualifications learners need to have before starting the course.
- Any particular skills or aptitudes learners need to help them participate successfully.
- What hardware and software learners require access to.
- What they will need to do to complete the course successfully.
- The assessment criteria and, briefly, how these can be met.
- If appropriate, when the course will start, and what deadlines learners will have to meet.
- How many hours they will need to allocate each week.

COSTS AND EQUIPMENT

There are a variety of costs associated with online learning. These could include:

- course fee plus examination entry fee;
- equipment costs, if learners do not already have access to a computer;
- Internet access costs, which might include a modem, plus subscription costs, plus telephone costs;
- new or upgraded software;
- the purchase of course materials other than those on the Web, such as print or video;
- tools and equipment associated with the course they are undertaking.

You could also point out that though learning online may be expensive, costs associated with face-to-face learning such as travel costs, loss of earnings, child care, etc. will not be incurred.

On this first information page you will also need to tell learners how to register for the course. You can include an online enquiry form, which will allow learners to receive additional information, or an e-mail address. Some learners may prefer initial contact to be via snail mail or phone so include those contact details too.

TECHNICAL SKILLS

Unless teaching any of the skills below is the aim of your course, your learners should already be able to:

- use a computer with confidence;
- input text efficiently, either using a keyboard or voice recognition software;
- access the Web using a browser;
- locate information using search tools;
- use e-mail, including sending attachments and setting up personal group e-mail lists;
- solve simple technical problems.

Learners may also need to know how to download and install software.

SELF-MANAGEMENT SKILLS

Learning online requires self-discipline. Your learners should be prepared to:

- log on regularly – at least once a week;
- deal with e-mails promptly;
- complete all required activities, exercises and assignments;
- be aware of deadlines and meet them or, if a deadline is missed, give reasons;
- work cooperatively with other course members;
- be open with the tutor or others about any difficulties they may encounter;
- plan their workload so that they have time during the week to undertake what is required of them.

Information about the course, costs and equipment needs to be available at the first point of contact. Discovering whether the potential learners have the right technical and management skills can form part of the guidance process. In any pre-course communication encourage your enquirers to be honest about the skills they have, and the time they are prepared to commit. Perhaps ask them to undertake some sort of pre-course activity that will assess their skill level. If you feel they are not prepared for the course then be clear about what skills they need to develop before they can undertake the course. Remember that if you enrol learners who are unready, it will waste your time, their time and money, and the time and money of other learners who have enrolled on the course. It does a disservice to all and your course and its reputation will suffer. It is your responsibility to do all you can during the recruitment process to ensure that you have a cohort of learners who have a clear idea of what they are undertaking, and that they bring with them the right level of ability and skills.

11 SUPPORTING LEARNERS THROUGH THE COURSE

The role of the tutor during an online course

The role of the tutor is somewhat different in online delivery. The body of knowledge that your learner must acquire will probably have been incorporated in your web site – thus the learner has access to it from the start. Lecturing is not part of the job that you need to do. Instead your responsibility is to guide your learners through the course so that they complete it successfully. Your job is therefore to:

- welcome learners;
- encourage and motivate;
- monitor progress;
- ensure learners are working at the right pace;
- give information, expand, clarify and explain;
- give feedback on learners' work;
- ensure learners are meeting the required standards;
- ensure success of conferences;
- facilitate a learning community;
- give technical advice and support;
- end the course.

If you think of your role as part teacher, part party host and part sheepdog, then you will have more or less the right approach!

Welcoming learners

For many learners your course will be their first experience of online learning. They are likely to be approaching the course with some trepidation. They will have little idea of what to expect or what will be expected of them, and they may well be nervous about whether their level of technical ability is sufficient to cope with the course. Ideally you should start the process of welcome and reassurance before the course even begins. It is extremely important that their first communication from you is reassuring and friendly. As soon as you know the e-mail address of your learners send them a friendly and personal e-mail which will assure them that the tutor they are dealing with is a helpful and approachable human being and not an electronic automated response system. Tell them a little bit about the course and what is likely to happen at the start of it, and ask them to respond to the e-mail so that you know that you have successfully made contact and that they can reply. An e-mail like this would set the tone:

Dear Philip

Welcome to the Report Writing course.

I will be the tutor on this course. My name is Marge Barker, and I have taught English and Communications at this college for seven years, and taught this particular online unit for the past two years.

The course itself will start at the end of this month. About a week before the course starts I will send you full details of the web address where the course is located and the user name and password you need to access it. Once the course starts you will be allocated to a study group of three or four people with whom you will work throughout the course.

I note from your registration form that you live in Glasgow. I visited Glasgow with my husband about six years ago and loved it. You are lucky to live in such a beautiful and culturally vibrant city.

Please reply to this e-mail so that I can be sure I have made contact with you. And please do not hesitate to contact me if you have questions about the course.

I look forward to working with you.

Marge

(include information here about how Phillip can contact you if e-mail is a problem)

Expect to receive a response to this e-mail within a week and if you do not hear from your learner then ring or write to him or her quickly to check that you have the correct e-mail address. It is extremely important that tutor/learner communication is established before the course begins.

COURSE START INFORMATION

Once e-mail communication has been established, follow up with any details that learners will need to access and undertake the course. These can be sent as a plain e-mail, as an attachment or in hard copy by post. Include the following information:

- The URL (web address) of the server where the course materials are located.
- Any user name or password, if the course web site is password protected.
- The e-mail address of the tutor.
- Alternative ways to contact the tutor (address, telephone or fax number) if for any reason e-mail contact has broken down.
- Any other relevant e-mail addresses (for example the course administrator, the course leader or technical support).
- The timetable for the course, including the start and finish dates.

A day or two before the course starts e-mail the learners again to remind them that the course is starting, and remind them of their first deadline.

STUDY GUIDE

It is a good idea to develop a Study Guide for students. This can be sent in hard copy, or in a form that can be printed out by students. This Study Guide could include the following information:

- The course aims and expected learning outcomes.
- Details about the course content.
- Advice that will help students manage their learning successfully, such as:
  - organizing their e-mail structure
  - backing up work they do
  - saving the course materials locally
  - any deadlines, and the implications of not meeting them.

- Any specific software they might need, and where they can get it.
- The methods that will be used to assess their work.
- What requirements they have to meet to ensure that they gain any qualification or credit.

LEARNER EXPECTATIONS

At an early stage of the course you should make sure that learners know what is required of them, and you should also ensure that they have a clear understanding of what they should expect from you and from the course. As is so often the case with online teaching, what constitutes good practice face to face is also good practice online. Thus, depending on the nature of the course, there may need to be some discussion and negotiation about what exactly these expectations should be. In a face-to-face course this would take place at the beginning of the course, partly involving the whole group and partly in discussion with individuals. In an online course you could conduct these discussions in the conference or by e-mail. This process in itself will be useful in introducing yourself to the learners, building up a sense of group and establishing the tone for communications.

What you may expect from learners is that they:

- log on to the course frequently;
- respond quickly to e-mails;
- communicate with other students on the course respectfully;
- inform their tutor and other students if they are having problems of access, or if they are going to be off-line for any period;
- accept that there may be occasional technological problems during an online course.

What students should expect from course materials is that they:

- are accurate in their content, their spelling and their grammar;
- are up to date;
- are written in a clear and unambiguous way and at an appropriate language level;
- have a clear navigational structure;
- are linked to appropriate external materials;
- are checked regularly to ensure that external links work.

What learners should expect from their tutors is that they:

- have expertise in the subject matter of the course;
- respond to any communications quickly (say within 48 hours);
- respond to any learner's work with detailed and constructive feedback (say within two weeks);
- create a climate that allows learners to learn independently and confidently;
- create a structure and a climate that encourages the development of a learning community;
- lead in identifying goals for the group;
- negotiate individual goals so that each individual has a personal learning plan;
- provide a structure that ensures that learners can succeed, for example by having review points when the tutor and learner can discuss their progress towards course learning outcomes and personal learning goals.

What learners should expect from the providing organization is that it:

- has a technological infrastructure that will, as far as reasonably possible, provide smooth and continuous access to course materials;
- will inform learners in advance if for any reason access to materials is likely to be interrupted;
- will keep learners informed about why access is interrupted and when the problem will be rectified, if advance warning of interruption is impossible;
- will provide a speedy and efficient administrative service.

Encouraging and motivating

Your learners will be on a steep learning curve. Not only have they embarked on a new course, but they will have to cope with technologies with which they may not be completely familiar, and which may fail from time to time. They may be experiencing distance education for the first time. All your communications with them must be positive and enthusiastic, and you must be ready to sympathize if they are having difficulties. You should also be realistic with them about the fact that the technology will sometimes let them down. Inevitably they will turn to you for technical support which you should give if you can. Always be ready to find 'workarounds' so that communication can continue. For some reason some people think that communication other than via the Internet is taboo during an online course. Make sure your learners know that if a phone call, letter or fax is necessary, then it is acceptable.

Monitoring progress

Once the course starts you will need to ensure that the learners are progressing through the course at the expected rate. That is why it is important that your course has built in plenty of activities/exercises/communication points. Unlike in a face-to-face course, the only way you can tell if your learners are active and involved is by their communication with you. Ensure that your course requires some sort of contact either as an e-mail to you or as a message to a conference some time in the first week. If you haven't heard anything in the first week then e-mail asking why and if you still don't receive a response then phone or write. Please keep the tone of any of these messages encouraging – learners won't want to get the virtual equivalent of a blackboard rubber thrown at their heads! This sort of thing would do:

> Hello Phillip
>
> I was hoping to have received your first activity, the summary of the example report. Please let me know if you are not sure what is expected of you.
>
> If there is some other reason why you haven't completed this activity, such as a technical difficulty, please tell me.
>
> If there are no problems can you let me have this activity by the end of this week (Friday).
>
> Thanks.
>
> Marge

RESPONDING TO E-MAILS

Plan your week so that you can give some sort of response to e-mails quickly. When you go through your course in-box, reply immediately to any e-mails that require clarification about the course and its organization, about an activity or which need some sort of technical explanation. This is particularly important if the learner's progress is being delayed by a problem. If any e-mail needs more consideration or investigation then acknowledge the e-mail and tell your learner that you will get back to him or her soon. This speedy turnaround for e-mails is particularly important in the first few weeks of the course when learners may be anxious about whether you are receiving e-mails, and whether the work they are doing is meeting course requirements.

STORING E-MAILS

Remember that in Chapter 5 I suggested it is sensible to set up a hierarchy of folders so that you avoid having an ever-growing in-box. I would advise a folder for each learner at least, and you may wish to create other folders that reflect the organization of your course. For example, on the courses I teach I have a folder for each activity. Thus when I receive an activity and cannot give feedback immediately I can acknowledge the e-mail, then store the activity in the relevant folder till I have time to give it proper attention. If you are disorganized yourself, you will not be able to track your learners' progress and you will fail to spot quickly any learner who may be encountering difficulties.

RECORD-KEEPING

Your learners will be justifiably irritated if you ask them for work that they have already completed, so set up a system so that you record receipt of work as soon as it arrives. A sensible way to do this would be to create a group progress activity grid. This can be produced in hard copy or electronically (see Appendix D). It is a good idea if your learners also have an activity grid to complete.

Giving information, expanding, clarifying and explaining

This is, of course, what all teachers must do and it is therefore part of the online tutor's job. The difference is that in a face-to-face course when the teacher directly addresses the learner, he or she must listen and reply. However, in an online course such communication can be avoided by the learner simply ignoring the e-mail. It is therefore necessary to deal with sensitive topics tactfully to ensure that the learner feels that such dialogues are worth having and that they will lead to continued or renewed commitment. If an e-mail has to be critical of a learner's work or progress, always precede such criticism with positive reinforcement of what the learner has achieved, and end by being clear about what the learner needs to do to prevent further criticism. Make sure the learner knows that you are willing to discuss the problem and find resolutions that are mutually agreeable.

Giving feedback on learners' work

Soon after the start of the course you will begin to receive required assignments and activities from your learners. I know you will already have an e-mail structure in place to cope with this. Give feedback as soon as it is practicably possible – one of the advantages of learning online is the speed of response as compared with traditional distance education when weeks might pass between the posting of an assignment and finding out what the tutor thought of it. Think carefully about the feedback you give. There will be no accompanying tone or body language for your learner to interpret. Find something positive to say about any work your learner sends to you. And be honest – it is not fair to your learner if you accept work that does not meet the standard it should. If aspects of the work are wrong or missing, state this clearly. The speed of online exchanges means that you can encourage your learners to send you drafts of work in progress so they can check that their work is on the right lines. And if you are thinking that this is how giving feedback should be given in face-to-face courses then you are right. There is often not a great deal of difference – good practice in teaching is often the same in an online course as it is in traditional classroom teaching. Think carefully about where you want to post the feedback. You may be using a conference to conduct the course, but learners will perhaps prefer that feedback on their assignments is not shared with the whole group.

Ensuring success of conferences

If your course delivery makes use of any sort of conferencing system then you must ensure that the effectiveness of this resource is maximized.

HOW DO I ...?

It may well be that even a learner who is very experienced with e-mail and the Web may not have previously used a conferencing system, so any course must allow learners time to familiarize themselves with its features. Questions of the 'How do I...?' variety will inevitably arise so try out all the things that your learners will be expected to do so that you can answer such questions quickly. Have a 'How do I ...?' sub-conference and encourage learners to support one another. If anyone asks a question, never, never suggest the question is foolish or too basic or wasting your time.

ENCOURAGE LEARNERS TO CONTRIBUTE EARLY IN THE COURSE

Most of us have had the embarrassing experience of being silent in a meeting for a long time, and then cringing when everyone turns to look at us with surprised expressions when we do finally speak. Although the surprised expressions are mercifully unseen in an online conference, it is still difficult for learners to participate for the first time once the conference is in full swing. Make it a requirement early in the course that learners post a message that will not prove too difficult for them, such as a brief introduction. Let each learner know you have noted their contribution and respond to it, however briefly. It may be a good idea to include a test sub-conference which can be used for learners just to try things out and not worry if they get it wrong.

STRUCTURE THE CONFERENCE AND SUB-CONFERENCES

If you are the conference administrator then structure the conference logically. It will be extremely difficult for learners to participate in ongoing discussions if there is just one large conference. The list of messages will get longer and longer and the threads and sub-threads will get more convoluted until it becomes a muddle impossible to untangle. You must create sub-conferences with unambiguous names that reflect what should go in them, for example a sub-conference for each topic. Avoid sub-conference titles that are too general. Do not have too many sub-conferences at the start, but be ready to add sub-conferences as the course progresses. Try to avoid having more than eight sub-conferences at any one time – watch for conferences that are no longer in use and close them down or archive them.

Encourage your learners to make sensible use of subject headings, whether in a conference or e-mail, and to be careful to post messages to the most appropriate sub-conference. Messages should stay with the point in the subject heading, and if the learner wishes to digress then he or she should start a new message with an appropriate subject heading. Messages should not be too long (one or two screens maximum). Messages of the 'I agree' and 'Me too' variety which do not move the discussion forward in any way should be discouraged (unless you feel that it may be that learner's first tentative step into a conference).

POST MESSAGES YOURSELF

Post a message to each sub-conference explaining how it should be used. You could perhaps use this message as an example of what you are expecting in terms of tone, message length and style. Remember that reading from the screen is more difficult than reading from the page, so keep sentences and paragraphs short.

Creating a learning community

Successful conferencing is not only about making sure that the structure is in place and that the learners are confident with technical aspects of its use. It is a place for human communication and interaction and so it is also your role to facilitate and support that.

INTRODUCE A SOCIAL ELEMENT

At an early stage encourage your learners to interact socially. You could start off by offering some information about yourself, perhaps about your professional experience, your interest in online learning, your home life and your family, any personal interests or hobbies. This will make the learner trust your expertise and also see you as a sympathetic and approachable human being. Make it clear that your learners are also welcome to introduce themselves, though remember that some may not feel comfortable about sharing personal information. Some learners may wish to withhold such information until they feel more comfortable with the other members of the course, others prefer to maintain a clear distance between their personal lives and their on-course relationships. These individuals should be respected, so do not press people to tell you and the other learners about their domestic arrangements or personal interests. If you are using a conferencing system include a sub-conference for social interactions, the equivalent of the learner coffee bar, where those who wish can get to know one another and discuss things not directly related to the course. Here they can tell jokes, talk about films they have seen or what they have been doing at the weekend. Tutors sometimes like to give such sub-conferences informal names such as 'The Frog and Modem' or 'Browser Bistro' – deciding on a good name for this sub-conference could be left to the learners and act as an 'ice-breaker' at the start of the course.

ESTABLISH GROUND RULES FOR COMMUNICATIONS

You may prefer to impose ground rules yourself, or allow the group to discuss and agree what they should be. For some general guidelines about the netiquette of the Internet refer back to Chapter 5 of this book. The guidelines below work well:

- Log on frequently (you may choose to specify how often, say three times per week).
- Respond to messages quickly.
- Participate in conferences and discussions (again, you may choose to specify your requirement, say two messages posted per week).
- Be respectful of others' opinions.
- Disagree politely and without hostility.
- Sexist, racist or other discriminatory language is unacceptable.
- Complete all activities and assignments required.
- Meet deadlines.
- If you encounter problems tell the tutor immediately.
- If you are going to be 'absent' for any length of time tell the tutor/course members.
- If technical problems arise get them resolved quickly.

Remember that most of these guidelines should apply to you as well as to your learners. If you are going to be off-line for more than a few days, let your learners know in advance.

FORM LEARNING SETS

Whole group communications, assuming that there is a whole group of ten or more, can be rather cumbersome, even intimidating, so it is a good idea to form learning sets which can work together during the course. Three to five people in a learning set seems to work well. Avoid putting people into pairs because if one person leaves the course, or their progress is disrupted in some way, it leaves the other half of that pair with no one to interact with. There are various ways you can decide how to form learning sets:

- Pick names out of a hat.
- Balance a mix of experiences, backgrounds, gender, location and age.
- Put together people who share experiences, backgrounds and so on.

You also need to decide whether to keep the learning sets together throughout the course, or reform and regroup them at certain points. The workability of this depends on the length of the course. Changing learning sets in a short course is impractical since relationships may take several weeks to build. If your plan is to change learning sets from time to time make that clear at the start of the course. Unexpected splitting of learning sets may cause resentment. An alternative is to keep learning sets together for a whole course, but have specific activities that require learners to work with different people.

MONITOR LEARNING SETS

If a learning set is working well together then acknowledge that fact. Sometimes a learning set just doesn't 'gel'. If this is the case, then act quickly. First, you should try to make the learning set work, for example by participating positively in discussion so that they have a model of what the learning set should be doing. You could ask one member to take the lead on a discussion. You can e-mail each member privately and ask them if they think there is a problem, and what solution they can suggest. You may need to remind them that their non-participation in the learning set is impacting on the learning of other people. If all else fails then consider splitting the set. If your plan was to reform sets from time to time, then now would be the time to do it. If you want to keep learning sets together throughout, then put the learners into existing sets. Be sensitive, though. The existing set should be consulted, and the new member properly introduced and welcomed.

FACILITATE DISCUSSION

As in life, some people in the virtual world love to discuss ideas, others are reluctant. Here are some tips for facilitating discussion:

- Kick off new discussion topics by posing a view and asking for others' contributions. As ever online, clarity is essential. Start topics off in a way that invites discussion, rather than just agreement or disagreement. Thus 'What would be the effect on a middle income family of lowering interest rates?' is more likely to start a discussion than 'Would lowering interest rates affect a middle income family?'
- Don't feel that the tutor always has to take the lead. Ask learners to initiate discussion topics from time to time.
- You may wish to invite a guest speaker with particular expertise to join the conference for a limited amount of time, say a week, to answer questions or lead a discussion.
- Encourage participation. Some learners like to 'lurk', that is to read messages but not post messages themselves. Unless it is a requirement of the course, don't expect every learner to join in every discussion, but expect that every learner should join in some. Invite contributions from particular individuals – 'I know Rahiem has had experience in this field – what did he find?'. If still no response, then e-mail a learner privately and ask why they have not joined in.
- Deal tactfully with anyone who seems to be trying to dominate a discussion. Try to distinguish between the over-enthusiastic learner and the arrogant one and act appropriately by e-mailing them privately to tell them to hold back a little.
- Be ready to ask questions or make points to nudge a discussion if you feel it is moving into irrelevant areas, or if important points are being missed. However, don't feel that every interaction needs to be policed, allow learners the time and space to discover things for themselves.
- Reinforce good online interactions with praise when contributions are particularly enlightening or interesting. Learners like to be referred to by name – 'Thanks, Lee. I thought your point about the criticism of twin studies an excellent one.'

- Decide and make clear to your learners when perfect grammar and spelling are important and when they're not. Be tolerant of errors in contributions to discussions provided they are not a barrier to communication. Expect higher standards in assessed assignments.
- Don't feel that you have to be the expert at everything. Honestly saying that you do not know all the answers will encourage learners to participate honestly too.
- If a learner disagrees with your opinion, don't pull rank.
- From time to time summarize the discussion, or ask one of the learners to do so.
- If you feel a discussion has reached the end of its life, then close it.
- If people other than you and your learners have access to a conference, for example a course leader or a technician, then you should inform your learners so they know exactly who is reading their messages.

Ending the course

When the course is nearing its end there are duties to which you must attend.

- Ensure learners are on target for completing all their assignments to the required standard.
- Some courses require learners to pull together all the work they have done and present it in some way, perhaps in a portfolio. Make sure your learners know if this is the case.
- Some learners may be a little sad at parting with people they have got to know, even though they have never met them. Consider setting up a 'Goodbye' sub-conference so these feelings can be expressed.
- It may be possible for you to set up something that allows your learners to keep in touch with each other if they wish to, such as an e-mail discussion list.
- Say how you feel the course has gone, say what you thought were the strengths of that group and thank your learners for their participation in the course.

12 EVALUATING THE COURSE

Has the course been a success? I hope so, but in online education as in all things there is bound to be room for improvement. One of the best ways to find out how the course can be improved is to provide a structure for receiving feedback on it.

Informal feedback

Throughout the course communications from your learners will have alerted you to issues that now need addressing. Perhaps the course materials need some sort of re-ordering and rewriting. Perhaps some of the activities have not worked as well as you anticipated. As things arise throughout the course make a note of modifications that can be made to improve the experience for your next and future cohorts of learners. It may be a good idea to have a course feedback sub-conference so these sort of issues can be raised and discussed.

Formal evaluation

At the end of the course ask your learners to evaluate the experience. You may well get a more honest response if the feedback goes to someone other than you, their usual tutor. Areas that should be covered include the following.

QUALITY OF PRE-COURSE GUIDANCE

- Were contact details included?
- Was information about joining the course clear?
- Was there a clear statement about course aims?
- Did you know what to expect, and what was expected of you?
- Were prerequisite skills and knowledge made clear?

QUALITY OF WEB-BASED MATERIALS

- Were these comprehensive and clear?
- Were they interesting?
- Was the style and vocabulary appropriate?
- Were they accurate?
- Were they free of grammatical and spelling errors?
- Was the path through the course materials systematic and clearly signposted?
- Were topics covered adequately?
- Were links to other sites included?
- Did they always work?
- Were these links well integrated and useful?

QUALITY OF TUITION

- Was the tutor easy for you to contact?
- Did the tutor respond to your communications quickly?
- Did the tutor respond to your communications effectively?
- Did the tutor have sufficient knowledge of the course content?
- Did you feel the tutor valued you as a learner?
- Did you feel the tutor treated you fairly?

COURSE WORKLOAD AND PACING

- Was the workload manageable in the hours allocated?
- Was progress through the course at the right pace?

QUALITY OF ASSIGNMENTS

- Were assignments well integrated into the course?
- Did assignments always contribute to the value of the course?
- Were there enough assignments? Or too many?
- Was it clear what was expected of you?
- Was tutor feedback on assignments prompt?
- Was tutor feedback enlightening?

QUALITY OF GROUP WORK

- Were group interactions encouraged?
- Did you feel able to contribute to group discussions?
- Did group discussions help you develop your skills, knowledge and understanding?

- Did your tutor facilitate group discussions?
- If there were communication problems, did the tutor act to resolve them?
- Was the conference structured appropriately?
- Was the conference managed appropriately?

TECHNICAL ISSUES

- Did you encounter any technical problems?
- Did any program cause particular problems?
- Were you able to get help to resolve technical problems?

GENERAL ISSUES

- Did you think the course was good value for money?
- Would you recommend the course to others? Why (or why not)?
- Did you achieve your aims?
- What elements of the whole course did you most enjoy?
- What elements of the course did you least enjoy?

Much of the evaluation could be done as an online form with the learner checking boxes (*Yes/No* or *Agree strongly* to *Disagree strongly*). Ensure that there is space for the learner to add additional comments, or to expand on a checklist point. Do not feel defensive. It is in your interest to know if your learners have not enjoyed the course or parts of it.

PART V

Appendices

Appendix A

CASE STUDIES

Case study 1: Study skills

THE BACKGROUND

For some years the Victoria College of Further Education had offered a range of courses that prepared adults for entry into Higher Education. These courses covered a wide academic area including sciences, humanities and arts, but they shared a core study skills course that all students were expected to complete during face-to-face tutorial sessions with their personal tutor. The study skills course covered such areas as:

- time management
- stress management
- research methods
- using libraries
- essay planning
- note taking
- revision techniques.

The students recognized the value of learning these skills, but since adult learners are frequently very hard pressed for time they sometimes felt that they should focus more on their main academic subjects.

The personal tutor team decided that it would be useful if the study skills unit could be delivered online so that students would no longer be required to attend a regular weekly time slot but could fit in their study skills development when it suited them. They, with guidance from their tutor, could decide what study skills they lacked, and the right point at which to acquire them. There would also be flexibility about where they studied – they could come into the college's learning centre, some would be able to access the course from a library or access point near their homes and a small but growing number had home Internet access.

DEVELOPING THE COURSE FOR ONLINE DELIVERY

Some of the planning work had already been done, since the job was to convert an existing course rather than develop a new one from scratch. The team knew how many students there would be, and the learning outcomes and the assessment criteria for the course were already in place.

The team split up the tasks that needed to be done in preparation as follows:

- Task Group 1: Reviewing the worksheets and handouts they already had to see if they could be used online.
- Task Group 2: Searching on the Internet and producing an annotated list of study skills sites for the tutors to look at and learn from.
- Task Group 3: Ensuring the college had a technological and administrative infrastructure that would support an online course.
- Task Group 4: Producing a checklist of skills that the tutors would need, and conducting a skills audit amongst the team.

When they met again they were fired with enthusiasm. The college was very supportive and agreed to allow some development time for staff and to pay for the services of a web page designer, and enough of the team had the Internet skills to pilot the course. Their review of existing online courses made them realize that just converting their handouts and worksheets to web pages was not the best way forward. They realized that they should now:

- decide on the structure of the course: what the modules should be and how long it would take a student to complete each one;
- adapt some existing materials and write some new materials that would be suited to online delivery;
- build in hyperlinks to external sites that would be useful for their students to look at;
- decide on what and when activities were needed so that tutors could be sure that students were progressing satisfactorily through the course;

- determine how the course should be organized in terms of tutor support and learner : learner interaction.

They decided to start off by developing just one module, on time management, which would then act as a model for the others. At this stage they also talked to the college web designer who worked with them to establish what the site could look like, and how what they wanted could be achieved technically.

PILOTING THE TIME MANAGEMENT MODULE

The module was mounted on the college's intranet and colleagues outside the tutor team were asked for their comments. This was an extremely useful stage in the process. The feedback made them realize that they should:

- rewrite some sections to improve clarity;
- change the look to make on-screen reading easier;
- improve navigation by adding a small link on each page that would take learners back to the home page.

The next stage was to pilot the module with a group of students. They carefully selected a group of students who had the right mix of Internet skills, academic interests, personal circumstances and Internet access. The tutor team learned a great deal from the student feedback from this pilot, specifically that:

- not all students had sufficient Internet skills to complete the module successfully;
- some sections still needed rewriting to ensure absolute clarity;
- some students found it a little difficult to find their way round the module;
- students with heavy demands on their time outside the course appreciated the flexibility it gave them;
- most students were surprised to find e-mail gave them improved access to their tutor;
- collaborative work was enthusiastically received;
- some students, but not all, found that social interactions emerged through the use of e-mail.

CONVERTING THE REST OF THE COURSE

On the basis of what they had learned from the pilot the tutor team felt they were able to convert the rest of the course. They had learned that:

- a checklist of skills necessary to do the course over the Internet was required;
- a short Internet skills course was needed for students who did not have those skills;
- course materials must be absolutely clear;
- navigation must be absolutely clear;
- tutors needed to organize their own timetables so that e-mail queries could be answered quickly;
- the number of collaborative activities should be increased;
- early activities should be incorporated to develop social interactions and group coherence.

Case study 2: Customer care

THE BACKGROUND

Alison Fowler is the training officer for a small but expanding chain of shops which sell outdoor equipment for camping and hiking. They have an induction programme for new staff which covers selling techniques, customer care, health and safety, stock knowledge, stock control, company background and structure, teambuilding and financial procedures.

The company started out with all its retail outlets within a 100 mile radius and it was easy for new staff to meet together for training days, and for Alison to visit the shops to give on-site training. The success of the company meant that this system was becoming increasingly impractical. An assistant training officer would be one solution, but this is something the company cannot yet afford. Alison decides to see if the situation can be eased using e-mail and the Web. The costs of this would be relatively small as all the shops have a computer and most of them are now online. The company sees the value anyway of using the Internet for communicating with its outlets and with its customers. Alison is very enthusiastic about online teaching, and she is a good trainer, but she hasn't had any experience of teaching online.

DEVELOPING AN ONLINE MODULE

Alison starts by reviewing the current modules and decides that she will create a new unit especially for online delivery which will cover elements of customer care, stock knowledge and shop procedures. The staff of each branch have a general knowledge of all stock, but individual staff are expected to be experts on particular aspects of the stock, for example camping equipment, walking boots, tents. It is important that new staff know who their branch's specialists are, and also that they begin to develop a field of expertise themselves.

Alison realizes that offering a course online will not work if the staff don't have basic IT skills, so she starts by sending a questionnaire to all new staff to ascertain their existing skills. She arranges for those staff who have some IT skills to go on a short Introduction to the Internet course and she also decides to test the new module on those staff first.

The outcomes she wants from the new module are:

- awareness of the areas of expertise that should be available in each store;
- knowledge of who are the particular experts in each store;
- exploration into possible areas of expertise that could be developed by each new member of staff.

PILOTING THE NEW MODULE

Alison begins by e-mailing her cohort, suggesting that they do some research on the Internet and send her an e-mail back with a list of web sites they think have information useful for their customers. Their replies make her realize that the question she asked was too broad as the sites suggested include some very sensible ones, such as advice for travellers about what injections they might need and another about walking holidays in Ireland, and some rather wild ones, such as one on line dancing and another that is just the web address of a search engine. She realizes that she will need to be a bit more specific. In fact in some cases she doesn't get a reply at all. She does not know whether some of the cohort don't have the IT skills after all, there has been a technical problem, or they simply haven't bothered.

Alison e-mails again. This time she attaches some guidelines to the e-mail for her cohort to print out and refer to while they are searching. She also gives them a deadline for returning the e-mails. This works much better. She receives some good suggestions for web sites, and once the deadline has passed the few who have not met it are telephoned to find out why. She also thinks that it is a shame that the information can't be shared. The word processor she uses can create web pages, so she puts together a list of sites found, mounts them on the intranet and informs her cohort. She receives several e-mails back saying how pleased they are with the site, and how it has interested other more experienced staff. She begins to think that perhaps working cooperatively would be a good way forward.

So Alison divides her cohort into pairs and gives them another task. This time she e-mails them a questionnaire which they have to print out and duplicate and use to find out the area of expertise of each of their colleagues, produce a word-processed summary, send it to her and to their partner, and then compare the range of expertise in their store with their partner's store to give them ideas about possible gaps that need to be filled. The task works very well in most cases, but a mild flu epidemic means that some people cannot complete the task because their pair is off sick. Alison decides to avoid pair work in the future and try groups of three or more next time.

The final activity of this module is for Alison's cohort to start thinking about what expertise they want to develop. She sends out a list of all possible areas of expertise and asks each of her cohort to e-mail her back with an idea for what they would like to research. The information from this exercise she uses to put people into groups of three or four and asks them to research on that particular field of expertise. They have to a) e-mail an experienced member of staff from another store with that expertise and ask them to list the things that they ought to know, and b) find useful web sites. This works really well. The cohort enjoy working as a group and, as well as sending messages about the activity, they begin to discuss other issues about working for the company such as exchanging ideas about successful selling and display.

REVIEWING THE PROCESS

In retrospect Alison can see that some of the mistakes made could have been avoided, but she feels that the experiment has been a moderate success. She has learned a lot, her cohort have enjoyed the process, some of the more experienced members of staff have been involved and interested, and she has acquired some useful information that could be shared with all staff.

She wants to run the module again, but decides she will make more use of the company's intranet. She designs a small web site with a page for each activity which explains clearly what is required, and each of these pages has some links to sites useful to support the activity. She decides to put the students into groups of three from the start so that they can give one another support, though the groups will be reformed for the final activity about the area of expertise they wish to investigate. She also decides to draw on the skills of experienced staff by including one in each group to give additional guidance and advice if needed.

Alison also realizes that although she has both good training skills and good technical skills, teaching online requires some special skills and experience. She decides to go on a course herself to acquire those skills.

Appendix B

SENDING ATTACHMENTS

Computer viruses

If you and your students are downloading programs from the Internet, or exchanging e-mail attachments, then there is a risk of viruses. Do not be over-fearful of these, but be aware that there is a potential danger and that there are simple methods for ensuring that you are not infected and that you do not infect other people.

WHAT ARE COMPUTER VIRUSES?

Computer viruses are small programs that reproduce by attaching themselves to existing programs on a computer. Their activity on your computer may not be immediately detectable. They are not accidental, they have been deliberately and maliciously developed to do harm. At present there are over 40 000 viruses and more appear every week. As well as receiving them from the Internet, you can get them from floppy disks that have been used in infected computers, or even from shop-bought software.

WHAT DAMAGE CAN THEY DO?

The type of damage varies from virus to virus. They may cause just a minor irritation such as flashing a message up on your monitor once a year. They may increase the size of your files which will mean the space on your hard drive will fill up. They may send out e-mails to addresses in your e-mail address book. They may reformat your hard disk, causing you to lose all your programs and saved work. However careful you are about backing up this will create an enormous nuisance to you.

HOW CAN I PROTECT MYSELF AND MY STUDENTS?

It is inevitable that in an online course you will need to exchange attachments so it is impossible for you to avoid the danger completely. You must obtain and use, and ensure your students obtain and use, up-to-date anti-virus software. Such software will perform regular checks on your computer (for example when you turn the computer on) and can be used to check disks and files before they are opened. Making use of such software is the only way to find out for sure that you have a virus. Since new viruses are always appearing your anti-virus software must never be more than three months old.

WHAT SHOULD I DO IF MY COMPUTER IS INFECTED?

Don't panic. Act immediately. If you fear that you may have infected anyone else contact them without delay so they too can take action. Run your anti-virus software to disinfect (as well as find) any viruses. Disinfecting a file may make it unusable, but better to lose one file than your whole hard disk.

WHAT ARE VIRUS HOAXES?

Almost as annoying as the viruses themselves are the virus hoaxes. These are e-mails that are sent round from time to time alerting you to some new, fictional virus. The e-mail will tell you some nonsense about what the virus will do and how to deal with it. Most importantly the e-mail will tell you to forward this information to all the people in your e-mail address book and therein lies the nuisance. If all these hoaxes were taken seriously then the e-mail system would clog up with everyone telling everyone else about these non-existent viruses. So how do you distinguish a real virus warning from a hoax? There are sites on the web devoted to virus hoaxes. A search using any search tool will locate these sites. Before swamping all your friends, relatives, colleagues and students with a warning, check out the authenticity of a virus warning at one of these sites.

Sending large attachments

The larger the attachment, the longer it will take for it to be uploaded and downloaded from the Internet. Text attachments, even long documents, do not take up many bytes, but programs and graphics do. You may want to exchange more than one file, for example the whole of a web site or a book divided into chapters. If this is the case then you should compress the file or folders first. To do this you will need a special program which will zip (compress) and unzip (decompress) these files and so will the person to whom zipped files have been sent. There are several available all reasonably cheaply and in most cases you can try out the software for free before you buy it. They are generally straightforward to use and need no special technical expertise.

If you wish to send graphics save them in a format that doesn't take up too much room, such as jpeg and gif. There may be some loss of quality but unless it is essential that the image is absolutely perfect then do not worry about it. There are various image editors available that will easily convert images from one format to another.

Appendix C

LEARNING OUTCOMES AND ASSESSMENT CRITERIA GRID

Unit title

Learning outcomes

Number	Details
1	
2	
3	
4	

Assessment criteria

Number	Details
1.1	
1.2	
1.3	
2.1	
2.2	
2.3	
3.1	
3.2	
3.3	
4.1	
4.2	
4.3	

Appendix D

GROUP PROGRESS GRID

Name of tutor: Start date of course: Number of learners:

Providing institution:

This record is for tutors to monitor learner progress through the course. It contains a list of all the activities, organized by unit and section, with the planned completion week for each activity. Insert the date on which each activity was completed against each learner's name.

Activity	Focus	Due end of week	Student name	1	2	3	4	5	6	7	8	9	10	11	12
Unit Number 1															
Activity number	Activity description														
Unit Number 2															

Appendix E

REFERENCES

Berge, Zane L. *The Role of the Online Instructor/Facilitator* (1996)
< http://cac.psu.edu/~mauri/moderate/teach_online.html>

Blackmore, Jessica *Pedagogy: Learning Styles* (11 August 1966)
<http://granite.cyg.net/~jblackmo/diglib/styl-a.html>

Felder, Richard M. *Matters of Style* (December 1996)
<http://www2.ncsu.edu/unity/lockers/users/f/felder/public/Papers/LS_Prism.htm>

Georgia Tech Research Corporation *GVU's 10th WWW User Survey* (Accessed 24 March 1999)
<http://www.gvu.gatech.edu/gvu/user_surveys/survey-1998-10/>

Glover, Dick *How do we Learn?* (August 1997)
<http://context.tlsu.leeds.ac.uk/MLEARNING>HTM>

Kaye, Anthony *Computer-mediated Communication and Distance Education* (Accessed 26 March 1999)
<http://www-icdl.open.ac.uk/mindweave/chap1.html>

Odasz, Frank *Online Teaching: A Significant New Pedagogy* (Accessed 9 February 1999)
<http://www.ed.gov/Technology/TechConf.odasz.html>

Paulsen, Morten Flate *The Online Report on Pedagogical Techniques for Computer-mediated Communication* (1995)
<http://www.hs.nki.no/~morten/cmcped.htm>

Rinaldi, Arlene J. *The Net: User Guidelines and Netiquette* (1998)
<http://www.fau.edu/netiquette/netiquette.html>

The Sheffield College *How to find Things on the World Wide Web* (29 April 1999)
<http://www.sheffcol.ac.uk/tools/search.html>

South Yorkshire Networks for Enterprise *Learning to Teach On-line* (May 1999)
< http://www.sheffcol.ac.uk/lettol/index.htm>

Zakon, Robert H. *Hobbes' Internet Timeline* (1999)
<http://info.isoc.org/guest/zakon/Internet/History/HIT.html>

INDEX